MICK CHANNON

MICK CHANNON

THE AUTHORISED BIOGRAPHY

PETER BATT

Published in 2004 by Highdown,
an imprint of Raceform Ltd
Compton, Newbury, Berkshire, RG20 6NL
Raceform Ltd is a wholly-owned subsidiary of Trinity Mirror plc

A catalogue record for this book is available from the British Library.

ISBN 1-904317-45-6

Designed by Fiona Pike
Printed by CPD, Wales

ACKNOWLEDGEMENTS

Without the generous assistance of Mick Channon's family and friends this book could never have come under starters orders. I thank them all and, in particular, Mick's eldest son, Michael junior, who partnered me from the stalls to the finishing post.

CONTENTS

INTRODUCTION

The first thing ace racehorse trainer Mick Channon ever asked me for was, believe it or not, a tip. He was a skinny, long-legged kid at the time when, uninvited, he sidled up to me one day and blew in my ear: "What's this old geezer Sir Alf Ramsey really like, then, Batty?" He had good reason to ask because he was just about to make his debut for the England Under-23 team, which, along with the senior England team, was managed at that time by the legendary old knight himself.

Now, if he had asked me which dog I thought was going to win the 7.30pm race at Walthamstow Greyhound Stadium that night he would have had more chance of a straight answer because in my own misspent youth I hardly ever missed a meeting there. In later years, I was to while away the time hanging on to Ramsey's coat-tails as a football reporter who travelled the world with England but as for attempting to tell young Mick all about Alf and then make sense of the answer, I would have had more chance of winning the Irish Lottery.

As sporting history has since recorded, the word enigma could have been invented especially to describe Sir Alf. If memory serves, I did say something along the lines that as far as I and most of my fellow football scribes were concerned he was the Prince of Darkness who treated us with about as much respect as he would a dog turd beneath his heel. Yet, at the same time, his chosen few – the England players – regarded him as some kind of Mother Teresa figure whom they could trust to cherish and protect them from their masters at the Football Association and the rest of the world in general.

As is explained later in these pages, Channon went on to become an England regular under the great man and it was he more than anyone who came closest to scoring the goal that would have saved England from crashing out of the World Cup against Poland at Wembley in 1973; such a goal would consequently have spared dear old Alf from the ignominy of losing his job.

Eighteen years later, I arranged to meet Mick and his mate and fellow ex-England international Alan Ball at the Cheltenham Festival to write an article about their joint soccer and racing exploits which was to be headlined "Channon and Ball" as a word play on the names of a couple of comedians who were the smash-hit celebrity funny men of their time. Unfortunately, it turned out that the only comedian around that day was yours truly and I was acting out a personal tragedy that could not have been a blacker comedy. Instead of making my deadline for the paper the journey to Cheltenham ended with me being hospitalised and then being stretchered off to an alcoholic rehabilitation centre from which I was to embark on a lifelong journey of a day-at-a-time recovery.

Fast forward through another decade – to 12 March 2002 – and I find myself watching Cheltenham with Mick and Bally on the television at Mick's home, whilst rattling a metaphorical begging bowl in the direction of his much sought after autobiography. Typically, this most generous-spirited of men then made a bit more sporting history than he already had done by agreeing to let me write this biography, for which he sacrificed so much of his precious time and then refused to accept a penny piece in payment. He has, however, instructed the publisher to donate an agreed sum to charity on his behalf.

CHAPTER ONE

THE WINNER IS...

Spent leaves flutter down to lie beside dead betting slips, turning the grandstand floor into a field of broken dreams. This is the last week of the Flat. This is mood indigo. There is still, however, more than a spark of life left in the 2003 season for two prominent racing men. They are Mark Johnston and Mick Channon, who are locked head to head in the struggle to finish as this year's top trainer in Britain.

One race is about to decide the outcome and it is being staged at Musselburgh, the little seaside course just outside Edinburgh that was once about as fashionable as a tartan cloth cap but has recently been modernised to such a lavish extent that it is staging the first ever Listed race in its 187-year history. It is being run over two miles and is called the Willie Park Trophy Stakes in honour of the winner of golf's first-ever Open championship as Park played his golf here at Musselburgh's links course.

Channon's Misternando wins it by three quarters of a length from Johnston's Scotts View and, in the process, stacks up enough statistics to satisfy even the most diligent of racing anoraks. His victory means that Channon has beaten Johnston with 140 winners to 139, Misternando has claimed the Channel 4 trophy as the horse that has won more races (10) than any other this season and his owner, John Duggan, is presented with an exact replica of the claret jug that is the prize for the golfers who win the Open. Misternando's jockey, apprentice Sam Hitchcott, has put so much gruelling effort into his finishing burst that he is stood down by the stewards for the rest of the meeting because they rule that he is exhausted and Channon has gone one better than last year, when he finished second to Johnston in the winning trainers' table.

This should have been the catalyst to send the champagne corks flying at Channon's stable down in Berkshire. All the more so since Channon had just beaten a man whom he gracelessly calls: "That bleedin' Jock". On the surface, the two men, "Jock" Johnston, a middle-class ex-veterinary surgeon and Channon, a working-class ex-scallywag of an English footballer appear to be poles apart.

In fact, they share the characteristic of being maniacs rather than mere addicts when it comes to that fashionable current malaise known as workaholism. For in the course of writing this book, yours truly – a mug punter of the old school who knows just about enough about racing to know that he knows nothing – has learned that it is a willingness to work far above and beyond the call of duty that separates the winning trainers from the losers. The "Jock" jibe from Channon is no more than an echo of this state of mind, a state of mind that was so graphically captured by the legendary golfer Gary Player, when he famously remarked: "The harder I work, the luckier I get." Gary is also now an extremely successful breeder of racehorses in his native South Africa.

Channon later follows up on the Scottish theme by saying:

"You know how much I hate the Jocks" but he is simply perpetuating the reputation for bravado that he earned back in his playing days when, after helping England to beat Scotland 5-0 by scoring his first full international goal at Hampden Park, Glasgow, in 1973, he enraged Scottish fans by his widely-publicised comment that the best thing about Scotland was the road back to England. He admits now: "That was just a wind-up but that was part of the fun of the game in those days, winding each other up. In fact, some of my best mates were Scots, such as Jimmy Gabriel, Jim Steele and Asa Hartford." His dig at Johnston is just a wind-up too, of course.

Mick was not even present at Musselburgh to witness his ultimate racing triumph. He had much more serious things with which to concern himself, matters that meant he was not even in the country. Instead, he was in the sunshine of Dubai comforting his wife, Jill, the mother of his two young children, just days after she had undergone an operation for breast cancer. Less than a week earlier, Jill had gone for a routine medical check only to be told that she needed an immediate operation and she was under the surgeon's knife within days.

"Obviously, it came as a terrible shock as we had no idea anything was wrong with her," says Mick. "By the time that Musselburgh race came along I had already whisked Jill and our two children off to Dubai to help her recuperate." Jill is his second wife and they have a ten-year-old boy, Jack, and a girl, India, who is seven. "We did not tell our children what was wrong with their mother because we thought they were too young to handle it," adds Mick.

"Because of the ongoing treatment we had to cancel the family's annual month-long holiday in Barbados, which meant that we would have no proper summer break this year," he explains. "Jill is being very brave and optimistic about the situation and we are confident that she will be fully cured but, as everyone knows, the chemotherapy treatment can be uncomfortable and depressing." Channon promises: "We will fight our way through this crisis in the same way that we fought our way to the top last season. Jill will keep turning up for the treatment just as my wonderful stable staff kept turning out runners.

"The other trainers must have been sick to death of us in the end. We were like terriers who wouldn't let go of their trousers. We turned out more than 1,000 runners and we turned them out in all types of races. A lot of moderate horses won for us and others just scraped home."

Channon modestly declines to add that he also hit the crossbar and the goalposts through having more second- and third-placed horses than anyone else. Or that the century of winners he registered was his second in succession. The horse that reached that particular milestone for him was a handsome grey that glories in the appropriate name of Compton's Eleven. Jointly owned by the late Paul Getty, Mick and the colourful ex-cricket captain of Hampshire, Colin Ingleby-McKenzie, it was named after that late cricketing icon Denis Compton.

"I was at the course to see that one win," says Mick. "I watched the race with my first grandson, Archie, who was only a few weeks old at the time. Many of Channon's other winners were far from the moderate lot he describes. His yard had two group winners, three Royal Ascot successes and were second in a Classic with Zafeen in the 2000 Guineas. But like Omar Khayyam's moving finger which, having writ, moves on, Mick is obsessed with the future and simply puts the past – whether good, bad or indifferent – down to experience. He says: "Needless to say, I was absolutely thrilled about last season's successes, but right now all I can think of is having Jill fit and well again and, work-wise, concentrating on the 100 or so two-year-olds we've just broken in for next season."

"Oh, and one other thing – collecting a monkey off my old mate and mentor Richard Hannon the next time I see him. We have a bet every year on who will train the most winners and this is the first time I've beaten him. Naturally, I'm hoping it will be the first of many."

CHAPTER TWO

ASCOT

If every life has a defining moment, Mick Channon's came on a Midsummer's Day at Royal Ascot when he rode down the straight mile in a royal carriage as the guest of Her Majesty The Queen. This was a scenario straight from the pages of a modern fairy tale – laced with symbolic sights and sounds that crowned the man's unique triumph of reaching the pinnacles of two disparate sporting careers. And if ever anyone is well versed in experiencing magic moments it is this extraordinary man. On the football field, he has scored winning goals for England and earned two winners' medals at Wembley cup finals whilst in horse racing he has trained more winners in a season than anyone else in Britain. The thing he remembers most about the day he made racing's most glamorous journey was that for the first seven furlongs the reverential silence was so eerie that he could have heard a lady's hat-pin drop.

His fifteen-stone body and rapidly balding head were dolled up in a morning suit and top hat and he recalls that he felt about as comfortable as a fish out of water. Then, as his carriage approached the grandstands, most of the punters thronging the cheaper enclosures began chanting: "One Mickey Channon, there's only one Mickey Channon" whilst the gentlemen in the Royal Enclosure raised their top hats as one with military precision and a few even shouted: "On me 'ead Channon, on me 'ead, son!"

The prelude to this momentous occurrence had come a few weeks earlier when a posh male voice on the other end of his telephone line invited him and his wife, Jill, to lunch at Windsor Castle with Her Majesty the Queen. His first instinct was that it was one of his best pals, either Alan Ball or Kevin Keegan, on a wind-up. The caller was just about to receive the kind of four-letter volley that would have made even Prince Philip or Princess Anne blush when some safety valve in his brain thankfully compelled him to hold his tongue. For the voice turned out to be the royal McCoy and its owner topped off the lunch invitation with a request for tea, to be taken in the royal box and, of course, that amazing coach ride.

As a country lad who was born in a thatched cottage and brought up in a council house on Salisbury Plain, Mick's first reaction was to address himself in the vernacular with an astonished cry of "Well, I'll be fucked!" He was as thrilled as he was flabbergasted. For, as a fervent royalist, he always nagged his fellow England players to sing the national anthem loud and clear during the presentations before international matches. And one of his most prized possessions is a photograph showing him, as the long-haired captain of an England soccer side, introducing Her Majesty to his team before the Silver Jubilee match against Scotland back in the 1970s.

The first thing he did when he put down the phone was to send a fax to Jill, who happened to be a guest at a friend's wedding in St. Lucia at that time, and simply say: "Would you like to join me for lunch with the Queen at Windsor Castle, darling?" Her response was to think immediately about a new outfit and then to contemplate having a nervous breakdown – in that order. She had five days in which to prepare but in typically feminine fashion her hat arrived by courier just a few minutes before the couple were due to leave the house for the big day and this understandably left her husband in a more agitated state than he had ever been in before even the biggest of matches.

Jill remembers: "I bought the most expensive outfit of my life up until that time. It cost £1,000 and was designed by Tomasz Starzewski. Then it was off to Paul Treacy, the top London milliner, for a £600 hat, but this had to be dyed to match the suit and that was what caused the delay that Michael moans about. Mind you, I've got the hang of this spending lark since then."

Mick counters with: "When we arrived at the castle, Jill was in such a state of high excitement that she was almost sick with nerves. I knew that feeling from my own playing days so I tried to calm her with that old footballer's cliché about concentrating on every moment because it would all pass in a blur just like it did for me when I played for Southampton against Manchester United in the 1976 FA Cup Final."

Jill continues: "As we were a little early, an equerry took us on a tour of the corridors, pointing out the famous paintings for us. The castle had just been refurbished after the big fire there and it looked in pristine condition. Next, we were taken to the drawing room for cocktails, where we chatted with Harry Herbert and his wife Chica. Harry Herbert is the youngest son of the late Lord Carnarvon, who was the Queen's racing manager and who had a big say in influencing Mick's professional life as a racehorse trainer. Harry Herbert also manages two prestigious owning syndicates, Highclere Thoroughbred Racing Limited and the Royal Ascot Racing Club."

Jill, incidentally, is the only person who calls her husband Michael. "I can't stand Mick or Mickey," she explains. "Michael has a much classier ring to it and he always says I'm the only bit of class in his life, anyway." Maybe so, but if they could talk I'm sure some of the multi-million pound Channon thoroughbreds would have something to say about that! Mick interrupts and joshes: "Jill may be a classy lady but that didn't stop her feeling more nervous and out-of-place than ever when Chica casually remarked that she had been out riding with the Queen that very same morning – talk about getting off to a flyer! Thankfully, though, Jill soon discovered that this was Chica's first time at a castle lunch, too, and the pair of them kept each other company all afternoon and have become big pals ever since."

Jill takes up the narrative again: "When the Queen, the Queen Mother and Princess Margaret had joined the party, we were all ushered into lunch in the white dining room. There were about two dozen of us at the table and equerries had obviously been discreetly dotted about between the guests to make everyone feel relaxed and comfortable. Michael and I were seated well away from each other, so it was definitely every man and woman for him and herself."

Says Mick: "Every time I glanced Jill's way I could tell she was feeling as highly strung as an unraced two-year-old at the starting gates." Explains Jill, "That's because we had been gently warned that proceedings for the whole day had to be synchronised down to the last detail and it soon became apparent that if you had not finished your food when it was time to leave the table then it would be hard cheese as far as the rest of your lunch went."

As for Mick, he spent most of the meal chatting with John Howard, the Prime Minister of Australia, who was seated next to him and was the only male present dressed in a lounge suit. Mr. Howard explained that he had been to see the Queen on business that morning – at which point I made a mental note that Her Majesty must be even busier than I normally am – what with horse riding and business meetings all before lunch," explains Mick. "Mr. Howard seemed to know a lot about my football career. This both surprised and flattered me as most Aussies of my acquaintance were either rugby or cricket crazy.

"I could only think that one of those helpful equerries had marked his card about me beforehand. Whatever ... he certainly gave an impressive and informative exhibition of an ace diplomat at work by paying attention to minor details like mine when his main concerns were with the great global scheme of things. And if I had learned anything in my few years as a trainer up to that time, it was that diplomacy was going to be an absolutely essential skill when it came to keeping a diverse group of owners happy or, if happy was too much to hope for in this, then, at least, reasonably contented with my efforts on their behalf."

During the pauses between conversation, Mick could not resist stealing wide-eyed glances at the Queen, Princess Margaret and, of course that great racing fan the Queen Mother. And, for some strange reason, which he suspects was buried somewhere in the quirks of his childhood, he found himself repeating, under his breath, the timeless words of that age-old nursery rhyme: "Pussy cat, pussy cat, where have you been? I've been to London to see the Queen." Mick continues with a laugh: "And then I thought: 'So you have, my son. So you fucking have!' "

Then he adds: "Fiddling nervously with the cutlery in front of me, trying to work out the correct running order of the knives, forks and spoons, my mind took me back to the first meal I ever had outside of my mum's kitchen. It was in a down-market, dockside boarding house where I was in digs when I was a 15-year-old apprentice with Southampton Football Club. I was nervous for a much more fundamental reason back then. For

I knew that if I lifted my eyes from the plate for more than a split second, one of the other scallywags around the table would take advantage of being on the landlady's blindside by forking off either my sausage or half a dozen chips before I could shout 'foul.' Retaliation would have brought only more pain because most of my dinner companions were hulking great stevedores or musclemen from the meat market. Still, practising those primitive table manners did help to remind me to keep my eye on the ball at all times."

Mick was soon to learn, however, that when it came to that particular discipline, the Queen's corgis could leave him for dead. There were several of them near the table during lunch and they must have been watching their mistress throughout every second of that meal. The moment Her Majesty stood up to signal that it was over, they all rose too, and at a snap of her fingers they obediently followed her out of the room.

Mick takes up the story again: "There were four horse-drawn coaches laid on to take us to the course and Jill and I got into such a muddle as to who was to sit with whom that I ended up in the third coach and Jill in the fourth". As the horses clip-clopped their way through Windsor Great Park there were crowds of people waving at the procession, oblivious to the fact that it was raining hard. But Mick was struggling to enjoy the moment because he was frantic with anxiety that Jill had been left behind in the confusion at the start. His worries were unfounded.

And Mick is quick to acknowledge that the rest of that fabulous day belonged much more to Jill than to him. As she recounts: "Tea was taken at several different small tables in the royal box and I was invited to join the Queen at the 'top' table. I still blush with shame, though, when I recall my first attempt at making a significant impact on the chatting that was going on. Apparently, there was some discussion about the countryside demonstrators who were holding rallies in Hyde Park that week and I piped up that she must make sure that she didn't go to Harvey Nicks then. I was just about to rip my tongue out with the pastry knife when the Queen smiled at my foolish little quip, obviously sussing out right away that I was a typical townie.

"Unwittingly, I made up the lost ground soon after this, however, when, during one of those pregnant pauses, which are so unnerving, I changed the subject to yachts. I asked Her Majesty if she was going to Cowes that year and she reminded me that this was the year that Britannia was going out of service. Multi-billionaire John Paul Getty II had come to Her Majesty's rescue by loaning her his yacht as a replacement. Well, it just so happens that Nicola, Mick's eldest daughter from his first marriage, has worked on John Paul's yacht for the past ten years, rising from deckhand to purser and that her partner is the captain. And this provided me with a perfect talking point."

The next time Mick was to receive the royal summons, that kind of small talk was to be superseded by conversations of a much more serious nature.

CHAPTER THREE

DEAL

Again, it came via a totally unexpected telephone call. This time, the man on the other end of the line was the Queen's cousin, Lord Huntingdon, one of racing's most popular eccentrics and known throughout the sport as Willie Hastings-Bass. Willie had succeeded the legendary Major Dick Hern as the Queen's tenant at West Ilsley and had been very successful, too. His most notable achievements had been to win three successive Ascot Gold Cups with Indian Queen in 1991 and Drum Taps in 1992 and 1993. He surprised Mick by telling him that he was retiring and going off to live in Australia. Then he surprised him even more by asking him if he fancied buying the stables.

To an aspiring racing man like Channon, that question was tantamount to: "Do you fancy winning the lottery?" The difference here was going to be the price of the ticket. That, Mick assumed, would be way beyond his financial reach. He vividly remembers his own reaction to the call. "Willie heard my gasp of astonishment followed by a long pause and then my answer of:

'Who wouldn't?' But I couldn't possibly afford it.' "

Undeterred, Willie kicked on with: "One of your sheikh owners might be able to help you out. Just come over and have a look." Mick says: "I started to think to myself that perhaps a peek wouldn't do any harm but then Willie virtually fucked up his sales pitch by asking: 'Why don't you bring Jill over, too?' For, much as I love Jill and I know she loves me and wants the best for me, I knew that she would put the kibosh on a grandiose scheme such as this. There was no way she would leave our house in Lambourn. She is an ex-interior designer and had only just finished lovingly fashioning it for herself and our two young children, Jack and India. We were all very happy living there and that house was her pride and joy. Everybody in Lambourn village commented on how lovely it was."

Like her husband, Jill, who was once an air hostess on Concorde, is nothing if not game and, after much pleading on Mick's part, she eventually agreed to take at least a look at West Ilsley even though she did regard it as just a quaint old racing museum-piece. Worryingly for Mick's hopes, she was right about the most important consideration from her point of view. For there was nothing remotely contemporary either about Hodcott House, the run-down old edifice that overlooked the stables and in which Jill and her children would be expected to live.

As Willie showed them around the place, he kept stressing its historical significance and every successive word made thoroughly modern Jillie wince, especially when she was told that some of the ancient titbits that had been found in the environs of the house would not have been out of place in a horror movie. Among the relics that had been uncovered during its various redevelopments over the centuries were a human skull under an original spiral staircase and a headless skeleton in the old garden.

She was also handed documentary information to the effect

that the original manor of Hodcott was mentioned in the Domesday Survey, was held by Ralph De Mortimer in 1086 and that it remained with that family until 1425, when it passed to Richard Duke of York and that the crown "became possessed of it in 1497". At this point Mick started to have misgivings of his own: "As a kid who was born in a thatched cottage on Salisbury Plain and then brought up in a council house this was all starting to do my brains in, too."

The briefing started to get a little less scary, however, when it was revealed that this admittedly archaic but nonetheless imposing building had been rebuilt in 1820 after a fire had destroyed the house that had previously stood on that spot and that had been designed in the Jacobean style by Inigo Jones. Local historians reckon that it was a beautiful villa then – until the Victorians had their go at it and turned it into something of a mishmash. It had a narrow corridor running right through it, so that viewing the ten bedrooms and four bathrooms was a bit like popping in and out of the different compartments in an old-fashioned railway carriage. It did have, though, enormous potential for redevelopment. Here was a virtual rabbit warren that with Jill's talents could be turned into something approaching a stately home. It was also obvious that this dark, gloomy old house would need a small fortune thrown at it.

To make matters worse, there was a lake immediately in front of the house that would have been unsafe for the Channon children, who were both still toddlers. If this were to be filled in, along with all the structural changes that would have to be made to these living quarters, it would need an army of builders and expensive modern equipment to do the job. So just one more sideways glance at Jill's shocked face was enough to tell Mick that he was a non-runner as far as West Ilsley was concerned. This did not stop him from having a wistful look at what he was going to be missing, however, and what was on offer work-wise was enough to satisfy any trainer's wish list and then some. There were 117 boxes, 196 acres of private winter and summer gallops, including one six-furlong, all-weather surface, a one-furlong, covered exercise ring and numerous barns. There were no fewer than 13 bungalows, two houses and a couple of flats on offer – all of which would, of course, complete Mick's rags-to-riches rise from a council-house kid into a country squire.

"Willie and I never even got around to talking turkey for the simple reason that I assumed the kind of telephone numbers required here could be nothing but dreams of avarice on my part," explains Mick. "But a few days later, Lord Carnarvon, himself, rang me up and asked me if I had liked what I saw and was I interested in buying? My answer to the first question was a resounding 'yes' and to the second a reluctant 'no'. His Lordship must have sensed what my mixed emotions were from the tone of my voice. And he simply said: 'Put in a bid.' This, of course, got me right at it again and I could not disguise my enthusiasm even to Jill, but she still thought it was all still so much pie in the sky, really.

"Then Lord Carnarvon rang again and said: 'What happened to your bid?' This time, I told him West Ilsley was way out of my league. He just repeated mysteriously, but firmly: 'Put in a bid.' So I did. And to my astonishment, negotiations began soon after this. These were conducted by my accountant, Jon Lisby, and my bank, of course, and by the Queen's land agent, Richard Morris, and by the keeper of the privy purse.

"Jill, bless her, made just one stipulation in all this and that was that whatever funding I could get for the deal a major part of it would have to be spent on the house. All I could do at this stage was to keep pinching myself and trying to read the minds of the Queen and Lord Carnarvon. I could think of only two reasons for the sale and, the more I thought about it, they were both very likely motives. The first was that Her Majesty was afraid that the stables would be lost to racing and that property developers might get hold of the land for housing. And the second was who else but me was there as a likely buyer. For by this time I had become one of the few trainers with enough horses to fill the boxes. You could count the rest of the possible runners on one hand and they were already spoken for.

"I was probably right on both counts because – with a little bit of give and take on both sides – the deal went through with no more tension than if I was watching one of my horses win a selling race. Later on, I was to discover that the Queen must have been as pleased as I was with the outcome. Whenever she sees me at the races now she always greets me with a warm smile and asks if everything is going well at the stables."

Coincidentally, Mick ran into Willie Hastings-Bass again at the Royal Ascot meeting in 2003, when his Lordship was on one of his frequent excursions from Australia. "You can't help greeting him with a warm smile – he is such a lovely fella," says Mick. In addition to being an amusing eccentric, Hastings-Bass has always had more than a touch of social conscience about him. He once cycled across a South Sea island for charity and, after the Bosnian war, he drove a lorry full of foodstuffs and other supplies to the Balkans.

"I sometimes wonder if he regarded Jill and me as charity cases when he was showing us around his old house," smiles Mick. "On the day Jill and I went to view there was a whole load of young Australian backpackers kipping all over the place there. And he was so laid-back about the whole business. The longer Jill's face got with disappointment at what she saw, the more he seemed to smile benevolently. Mick recalls that he tried to cheer Jill up by asking Willie to show her the back garden.

"Well, as I opened the door, the biggest swarm of bumble bees you've ever seen in your life started dive-bombing us and whizzing around our ears. Jill was terrified and I wasn't best pleased either. But Willie just smiled serenely as if this was an everyday happening. Then he stated the obvious by informing us that there was a bees' nest just above the back door. And when Jill said, as politely as possible, that we would have to do something about that, Willie looked aghast and said 'Oh no, just think of all the cross-pollination you could get.' "

Mick regards Lord Huntingdon as one of those life-changing catalysts that keep turning up in a person's life when you need them most and even when you least need them. He explains: "I first got to know Willie in Australia when I was playing for a team called Warwick Farm and Willie was always backwards and forwards between Blighty and Aussie. At that time I was on what you would call the slippery slope but what we old pros called 'the glass mountain'. I was prostituting myself at the end of my career and earning a few quid for the rainy days that seemed to be coming. So maybe my old 'agony uncle' remembered those days, too, when he persuaded me to buy West Ilsley.

"And, would you believe, he still keeps turning up here from time to time, telling me how to prune the trees and tend the garden. A while ago he came here with a few American chums who were potential buyers of some of my horses. He promptly went missing and we had to send out a search party of stable lads. They found him, camera in hand, like some sort of spy, snapping away at everything. When I asked him what he was up to he said he was taking pictures for the boss (meaning the Queen) and that he was going to send them to her on the internet because she still loves the place.

"I felt the need to tell him that I was the boss now, but I did not feel so cocky a few days later when Lord Carnarvon asked me to come and chat with the Queen at Newmarket races. She asked me how things were progressing at the stables and I had to confess that I had upset a few of the locals in the area because some of my lads had got pissed and fallen in the village duck pond.

"She said:'So I've heard' and then she advised me not to worry too much about it because a similar thing had happened with Dick Hern's lads in the old days.

"The first thing I did when I got home that night was to phone my mum and dad and tell them that I was moving them from Salisbury into one of my bungalows at West Ilsley. I had fully intended to do this from the day I moved in, but that reminder of the goings-on at the duck pond made me realise that they would bring an air of respectability to the place as well as their love and kindness."

By then, Jill had hired an architect, structural engineers and builders and spent ten months going backwards and forwards from Lambourn to West Ilsley every day. She is now able to describe Hodcott House as her "dream home".

CHAPTER FOUR

STABLES

The West Ilsley stables were a very different proposition to Hodcott House. Jill, like everyone else who first claps eyes on them, had to admit that they were situated in God's own country, nestled as they were in the centre of the beautiful Berkshire Downs. In spring and early summer there is no setting more glorious in which to start a working day and on such mornings Mick Channon feels he is taking a liberty by just being alive. The breaking dawn paints the gallops gold, the air is crystal clear and the silence is broken only by birdsong. But on most mornings when I've been there this soothing scene is suddenly vandalised by the raucous Wiltshire twang of the trainer who is swearing non-stop at the work riders. This industrial language is not the only relic of Channon's earlier life as a star footballer. He is limping heavily, too, half crippled by his old football injuries, and he has zoomed up the handicap weight-wise, through having to hump around at least four stones extra these days.

As the string snorts past, you can feel, almost as intently as their riders can, the hot, sweet breath flooding up from the dark wells of the nostrils of nature's most wondrous creation, the thoroughbred racehorse. You know precisely why the Queen chose to stand here on so many occasions when she owned the place. If you let out enough rein on your imagination you can see the Duke of Cumberland exercising his horses here hundreds of years ago and then strain your ears even harder than your eyes and you can pick up distant echoes of the sound of King Alfred and his warriors locked in battle with the Danes much farther back in time on this selfsame turf.

Trainers prepared thoroughbred horses here throughout the 20th century, beginning with Frank Barling, who was resident during its first two decades. West Ilsley's twin village of East Ilsley, a mile and a half away, has been the home of thoroughbreds for even longer. For instance, a horse named Lord Lyon won the Triple Crown for trainer James Dover as long ago as 1866 and its present trainer, Hughie Morrison, is firing in winners on both on the Flat and over jumps. But West Ilsley did not really become the stuff of racing legend until Major Dick Hern set up shop there in the early 1960s.

In Hern's day the boxes housed such illustrious colts as Brigadier Gerard, Bustino, Henbit, Troy and Nashwan and the flying fillies Dunfermline, Bireme and Sun Princess, to name just a few of the superstars that were readied here by the incomparable major. These nameplates and others almost as illustrious still adorn their former boxes. But surely the most poignant tribute ever paid to this magical place came when Buster Haslam, Dick's long-serving travelling head man, hanged himself down at the boxes known as the stud because he could not bear the thought of leaving West Ilsley when the major was forced to vacate these precious premises in 1990.

The controversy surrounding the termination of the Major's lease by the Queen's racing manager Lord Carnarvon, after Dick had been crippled by a hunting accident and then laid low by heart surgery, has been the subject of so many column inches in both the racing and the national Press that there is little point in repeating it in great detail here. In brief, in 1988 Dick Hern was informed by Lord Carnarvon that his lease, which was due to run until 1990, would not be renewed due to Hern's ill-health. Then, he recovered sufficiently well to train Nashwan, winner of the Guineas and the Derby in 1989. This triumph still came too late to save him, despite some furore from the public and the press. When asked for his views on the matter, Channon simply pleads that hackneyed but nevertheless valid cliché about taking people as you find them. And he adds that in his dealings with both the late lord and the late major he received nothing but courtesy and consideration.

Local inhabitants are fond of repeating the story about the day they saw the Queen become a "temporary traffic policewoman". Her Majesty had been with Dick in his Land Rover when a green, two-year-old filly got loose at the top of the starting gate canter on the winter gallops. After a number of failed attempts to catch her, Dick decided to walk the string home, hoping that the filly would follow. The Queen, according to legend, went ahead to the crossing of the West Ilsley to East Ilsley road to control the traffic in case the filly took it into her head to gallop down the track towards the stables and then strayed on to the road. Fortunately, Her Majesty was able to "knock off early" when the errant young horse finally attached herself to the rest of the string and walked quietly home.

When Major Hern first moved in during the viciously cold winter of 1962, he was greeted by a carpet of snow lying nine inches deep on the Downs. It was in the depths of winter, too, that Mick first set eyes on these stables in 1996. But as far as he was concerned, it felt like June in January to be gazing at such an integral part of so many modern triumphs of the turf. And as far as the royal vendor's attitude? Well, Mick was as welcome as the flowers in May at the place.

For, as Harry Herbert, who is speaking from his ancestral home Highclere, explains: "Everyone was absolutely thrilled that Mick was the man who bought West Ilsley. It was very important that one of the most historic and beautiful stables in the land fell into the right hands. My late father was very fond of Mick and had the utmost respect for him. So much so, that when he was chairman of Newbury Racecourse, he set up a committee to decide who were the best two-year-olds to run at the track and Mick was one of the guys he chose for that job."

Herbert goes on to explain how the queen initially bought West Ilsley from Lord Weinstock, using the proceeds of the sale of her high-class mare, Height of Fashion, to Sheikh Hamdan. "And now Mick has Arab owners among his patrons," says Harry. But he is quick to acknowledge that Channon also embraces a whole Hogarthian landscape in the wide sweep of owners he accommodates. "It is thanks to Mick and some of his pals, like Richard Hannon, that racing has at last rid itself of so much of the old pomposity and arrogance that once riddled the sport. There is still so much rubbish talked in this industry, but not from the likes of Mick and Richard.

"These guys don't give a fig about your background. They judge you as a person. They don't care whether you've got a title or a million in the bank. And as everyone in racing now knows, Mick and Richard call a spade a spade and then some. You only have to stand next to Her Majesty when her horses are on the gallops at Richard's stable to hear the F-word flying about from time to time. And if the Queen ever has horses with Mick, which no doubt she will one day, she knows full well that she'll hear more of the same from him.

"And as for the competitive edge they bring to the game, you only have to board Richard's plane with him, Mick and Pat Eddery for company and by the time you disembark they will have cleaned you out at cards. They have a tremendous friendly rivalry and are always betting each other as to who is going to be the first to 50 winners and then a hundred and so on.

"Mick knows better than most than this is a numbers game. That's why he is never afraid to run his horses. Whether they cost five grand or a million, he is always willing to let them take their chances. That is why he is so successful with two-year-olds. And that's why he is being fed with the best that money can buy or breed now and he deserves it. I'm sure he'll be looking to win classics in future and I certainly would not put it past him to win the Derby one day."

CHAPTER FIVE

BREEDING

Outside of Greek mythology, Mick Channon must be the nearest thing to a centaur that the human race has yet produced. The only other two half-man, half-horse creatures that this country has managed to conjure up are Frannie Lee and Mick Quinn. Both, incidentally, are former team-mates of Channon's.

Lee, of course, played alongside Channon for Manchester City and England and became a racing trainer after making his fortune in business. He then enjoyed eye-catching success with the horses until he went for broke by buying and controlling City in 1994 before relinquishing the chairmanship four years later. Quinn played with Channon at Portsmouth and later became his protégé and pupil at the horse racing game where he is still struggling to make an impact after being suspended from the training ranks for two years for neglecting his horses' physical welfare when he went off on holiday.

There was once a time when football's only link with racing

was bored players blowing their wages in the betting shop after training. But in this more affluent age, dozens of big soccer personalities have joined the ranks of owners and breeders in the increasingly fashionable linking of the two sports. They include Sir Alex Ferguson, Kevin Keegan, Alan Ball, Peter Shilton, Alan Shearer, Terry McDermott, Michael Owen, Robbie Fowler, Steve McManaman, Dietmar Hamann, Stuart Pearce, David Dunn, Gary Flitcroft, Alan Brazil, Harry Redknapp, Paul Ince, Ally McCoist, Vinnie Jones, David Platt, Emlyn Hughes, Ian Rush, Jan Molby, Rory Delap and Seth Johnson. But none, to my knowledge, has yet shovelled shit and driven horseboxes as Channon, Lee and Quinn have done although a former non-league FA Cup giant-killer, Ricky George, once of Hereford United, managed to top the lot of them with his part-ownership of 1998 Grand National winner, Earth Summit.

No one else has either come or is ever likely to come close to turning out as many winners and scoring as many goals as Channon has in his truly remarkable double life. He has captained England, won 46 caps, won both the FA and Football League Cups, scored more than 300 goals and has twice trained more than 100 domestic winners in a single Flat racing season as well as numerous others abroad.

The only notable omission from his unique cv is the lack of a Classic winner. But do not bet against him doing that soon. He came within three quarters of a length of winning the 2,000 Guineas in 2003 when his Zafeen finished second, but he sums up that shot against the crossbar by saying: "I am not desperate. It is just a matter of time before I get my first Classic winner. With a fabulous set-up like this at West Ilsley we will have to get a few Classic winners to justify our existence."

It should come as no great surprise, then, to learn that Mick's favourite bedtime reading is the various books and brochures on breeding. But what surely is surprising is his revelation that on trips abroad with England and Southampton, he and Kevin Keegan often had their heads buried in Tattersalls breeding brochures. Yet, for me, the most fascinating form lines on offer are the ones that conspired to create such a hybrid creature as Channon himself.

An age-old sporting aphorism maintained that if you wanted to find a centre-forward (or a fast bowler) you simply whistled down the nearest coal mine. But in the light of more recent scientific studies in genetics it would seem that mum and dad would have a lot more to do with a boy's ability to bend it like Beckham than his everyday environment.

Well, a somewhat eccentric acquaintance of mine, Alan Brown, who was the celebrated manager of Burnley and Sunderland a few decades back, used to cut his theoretical cloth even finer than this. He started many a pub argument with his conviction that if male human athletes could be manufactured to order like racehorses, then the all-important genes for sporting prowess would be those bequeathed by the boy's mother. He could produce lists of famous footballers and their mums to prove his point. His own favourite example concerned the legendary Charlton brothers, Jack and Bobby, whose late mother, Cissie, was a member of the Milburn clan that boasted several top-class players, the most notable being "Wor Jackie" Milburn of Newcastle United and England fame.

To add weight to the flip side of Brown's highly debatable conviction, it has to be admitted that the roll call of famous footballers with famous footballing fathers is very slim indeed. And if any contemporary reader feels like trumping those cards with the names of Jamie Redknapp and Frank Lampard Junior let me confound some of them with the knowledge that their fathers, Harry and Frank senior, are married to two girls who are sisters.

At this point in the equation, blow me down if current bloodstock expert and owner Tim Corby, who has horses at West Ilsley, does not offer similar evidence regarding thoroughbreds. He insists: "The broodmare's line is vital in producing top racehorses. The most important ancestor is the mare's father. If the newborn colt's maternal grandfather was useless you've got no chance."

It so happens that Mick Channon got off to a helpful flyer on both sides of his pedigree. His mother, Betty, was the outstanding girl athlete at her village school nearly 70 years ago and his late father, Jack, ran away from home at the age of 15 to become a cavalryman in the British Army before the Second World War. But the biggest single factor in forging the man's psychological hunger for success surely came in childhood when, at the age of nine, he lost his 14-year-old brother in a tractor accident.

All these years later, Mick says: "There is never a day passes when I don't have fleeting thoughts of my dead brother, John. We were inseparable as kids and it still hurts like hell that he wasn't able to share in my good fortune. I sometimes think that it was having to listen to my mother's tears night after night for what felt like years afterwards that spurred me on to try to take her mind off the tragedy just a little bit by making a success of my life." He has not let her down.

Nor has he let down one of his oldest and most respected football pals, the aforementioned Frannie Lee. Recalling the pair's almost parallel lives, Lee, who is four years older than his mate, says: "Mick Channon stalked me all my life. He stalked me into the England team, he stalked me into the Manchester City team and he even stalked me into racehorse training."

They both made their first-team debuts as 16-year-old boy wonders (Lee for Bolton Wanderers) and Frannie played 625 first-class games, scored 297 goals and notched up 150 winners over both Flat and jumps in his eight-year training career. Lee's talking has always been as straight as his shooting and he makes no bones about it when he says: "Training a winner at the races gives you a bigger adrenalin rush than scoring a winning goal in even the most important of football matches."

Warming to the subject, he muses: "All I know is that if I ever come back here in a future life, I would like it to be as a champion racehorse. When a footballer finished in my day he had to scratch about looking for another living, but if you can go to stud as a great racehorse, you spend the rest of your days living in five-star luxury, you can have your wicked way with more mares than most men have hot dinners, you get someone to tease the mares for you and someone else even helps you to put your willy in – then if you're any good at it they fly you off to America or Japan to start all over again." And only half-joking, he adds: "I sometimes wish I had stuck to the horses instead of taking over City – at least the horses couldn't answer back.

"If they could talk they would tell you that equine and human athletes may be different physiologically, but in their physical and psychological needs they respond to roughly the same thing and that is loving kindness. You can talk about the theory of sticks and carrots all you want but deep down neither horses nor footballers really respond to the big stick. Every athlete needs his or her ego massaged and it's just having an instinct to know how to do this without losing control over them. Having been through the rigours of professional training like Mick and I have, obviously it helps us to understand our horses. We know that, just like our old football pals, the different physical types need to concentrate on different aspects of peak fitness such as speed, strength and stamina, which obviously vary from individual to individual."

Of his long-term mate Mick, he says: "I definitely think he has it in him to become champion trainer, he's turned out to be a genius with the horses. Incidentally, we spend every summer holidaying in Barbados where we both have houses. And Mick and Mike Summerbee were with me at my place when I clinched the deal to take over at City. We cracked open a few bottles that day, I can tell you.

"As for the training, I got brought down to earth by the dreaded virus which haunts so many stables at some time or another. I still have my stud, which I bought 26 years ago, but the virus struck my string around the same time as I was negotiating to take control of City and as I was and still am chairman of my own paper company, something just had to give and it was the racing. I still love the game, but the hardest thing about it is the amount of time you spend in traffic jams getting to and from the various courses. And that bloody virus really sickened me. It was bad enough having the odd barren spell when I was a striker, but seeing your horses keep blowing up about two furlongs from home really eats into your emotional well-being.

"It has to be said that the other downside to the training game is too many bad owners. There are not that many but even one or two is too many. I can tell you of cases where I've let them have my box at Haydock or York, which would have cost them £750, and they've had the nerve to moan when it came to paying a blacksmith's bill for £25. I shouldn't think my old mate Mick will have to put up with too much of that any more though because he really is in the Premier League of the racing game now and long may it last for him."

CHAPTER SIX

EARLY DAYS

Michael Roger Channon was the middle one of three boys, who, according to his mother, Betty, were the be-all and end-all of their parents' world. This is backed up by Mick's younger brother, Phil, who says: "During our boyhood, dad had two jobs. He drove a lorry for the army by day and worked on a farm in the evenings lifting hundredweight sacks of grain. We had to take it in turns to go up to the field with his tea. We now know that he did this so that us kids could have new football boots and the like whenever we needed them. He liked a drink but he even sacrificed going down to the pub with his mates at night so that we had some of life's little luxuries. But neither mum nor dad spoiled us, they were what today would be regarded as old-fashioned parents who made us learn right from wrong."

All three boys were born in a tiny, thatched cottage in the village of Orcheston on Salisbury Plain: John in 1944; Mick in 1948; and Phil in 1952. Phil describes their arrival in the world this way: "Dad had a habit of putting one of us in the oven every leap year. Dad died suddenly of a heart attack a couple of years ago but thankfully not before Mick had repaid him and mum in spades for those early sacrifices. As an old cavalry man, dad was as happy as Larry when Mick and Jill used to invite Major Hern and his wife to dinner and the pair of them yarned about their old army days.

"And dad's greatest pleasure later in life, when he and mum lived at West Ilsley, was to polish those brass nameplates of all those famous horses that the major had trained there. Whenever dad tried his hand at riding one or two of Mick's horses, though, that cheeky sod used to take the mickey out of the old man's upright, military way of sitting in the saddle. But one of the most touching things Mick ever did for him came after he died when he had a seat of remembrance built in dad's honour in the middle of the stable. And one of mum's proudest possessions is a photograph of some of Mick's old World Cup-winning mates of 1966 sitting on it together."

The Channon brothers grew up in the austere 1950s and, like millions of other working-class youngsters, it never crossed their minds that having an outside loo was in any way primitive. But Betty's obsessive dream was to have a "proper posh" bathroom. So the moment she heard that there were new council houses being built in their village with not just one but two toilets inside them, she put the family's name down for one, knowing that as lifelong residents in that area she and her husband were racing certainties to move "up market" as soon as the last bricks were laid.

Mick and his brothers did not share their parents' delight at this upheaval. "It meant that we had to give up our pet pig, Spud," Mick recalls. "As very young kids we were all potty about Spud and we made a permanent little pen for him at the back of our cottage. We even got dad to build us a little wooden trolley to push him around in and I must confess that I was reminded of this when I took that ride in the royal carriage at Ascot all those years later." Mr and Mrs Channon were quite naturally worried that their new neighbours might turn their noses up at Spud so the boys were forced to abandon their pet to what Mick describes as "the perils of Salisbury market".

Younger brother Phil describes the Channons' boyhood as "idyllic". He recalls: "We had the whole of Salisbury Plain as our back garden. Stonehenge was open to all and sundry in those days and we must have climbed every ancient stone there. As we got older and became more and more interested in football, though, we were like country boys in search of an inner city. The back gardens of our council houses nearly all had immaculate lawns in those days and the residents were much too proud of them to let their kids play football in the street. Now Salisbury Plain is all very well for playing football with pullovers for goalposts but if you wanted to shoot at goal hundreds and hundreds of times in the same evening, as Mick did, then you were in desperate need of something to stop the ball.

"We found our ideal goal in the shape of the only wall for miles around. It skirted the old rectory. So we chalked up goalposts there and the vicar lovingly let us get on with it even though the noise of the ball thudding into that wall must have driven him crackers. The fact that our mum made us go to Sunday school every week might have had something to do with his tolerance towards us, though," grins Phil.

All three Channon boys were natural athletes. "I think it came down from our mum," says Phil. "At school, Mick was good at everything like that: sprinting, long jumping, high jumping, even the pole vault and I'm told John was the same. I know that Mick looked up to John in every way."

But the one long-term memory that far outweighs all the others for both Mick and Phil, is, of course, the tragic early death of their brother. Phil explains: "I was only six at the time, so I can't recall everything about our lives then although I was told later by mum and dad that John's death sent Mick into his shell for quite a while. As for me, on the day we were told that John was dead, I have a photographic memory of the scene etched so indelibly on my mind that I could still draw our front room in every detail. That was where I heard the terrible news. Mick and I were being informed that John had been helping the local farmer when a tractor, loaded with hay, overturned and crushed him. I obviously couldn't take it all in properly but I can still vividly remember the carpet, the settee and armchairs, the mantelpiece and everything on it. I know exactly where everyone was sitting or standing and I can still see the expressions on the faces of my grandmother and my aunt.

"Mick had always been an extrovert – always on the go, always laughing but apparently he turned in on himself for a while. This seemed to make him totally focussed on whatever he happened to be doing. For instance, if he was reading something or watching television you could not grab his attention for love or money. He seemed to develop deep powers of concentration – perhaps as an escape from his thoughts of John. I think it was this tunnel vision that helped him so much when he became a professional footballer. As everyone knows, concentration is the number one requisite for any successful sportsman. I think this was the main difference between Mick and myself. We both played for Wiltshire schoolboys and I had a trial for the England youth team, but I lacked Mick's dedication to the game.

"My brother is not one of those driven personalities who must have success at all costs, though. It's just that he wants to try everything he takes a fancy to and then he wants to do well at everything he sets his mind to. His attitude has always been: 'If you don't buy a ticket, you're not in the raffle.' And when he is successful, he makes absolutely sure that everyone around him shares in that success, too." At this point in Phil's testimony he echoes a theme that is on the lips of everyone, but everyone, I have spoken to about Mick Channon, including myself. And that is that the man is incredibly generous – with his money, his time, his spirit and his loyalty. "I just can't speak highly enough of him as a person, let alone my big brother," says Phil.

When Mick moved from his village junior school to a bigger secondary modern, there was soon something else that everyone said about him, too: that he was head and shoulders above most other boys for miles around when it came to natural soccer talent. So, like almost every other soccer star before and after him, he was still in short trousers when the professional scouts came sniffing around.

Ironically, for a man who was to become a specialist in trying to pull off coups in the racing game and, like every other trainer, an expert at not letting his left hand know what his right hand was doing when it came to dispensing information, there was some cloak and dagger mystique attached to the circumstances which saw him sign on the line as an apprentice professional footballer. At first sight, the two big clubs nearest to Mick's home, Swindon Town and Southampton, both fancied the hell out of this skinny, sensationally swift-footed kid. Many years later, Mick himself also became a scout of sorts. He weighs up yearlings and two-year-old potential racehorses in the sales ring and can, with a little bit of help from his equally expert friends, usually tell if they will be able to do the business like he once could.

Bert Head was manager of Swindon Town when Mick was that sought-after schoolboy and, according to Phil Channon, told people later that he was sure he had young Mick in the bag. But the day before Bert went to do the persuading, Southampton beat him to it in what was virtually a photo finish for Mick's signature. "The Saints pulled a right stroke," says Phil. "They heard that Bert was aiming to sign Mick on Monday morning, so they nipped round to our house on the Sunday evening. The only problem with that should have been that it was illegal to sign schoolboys on a Sunday. They pulled the wool over everyone's eyes next morning, though, by staging a photographed signing session in a local café."

Mick himself recalls that big moment in his life like this: "The manager then was Ted Bates, who was to become a lifelong friend. His chief scout, Tom Parker, had first recommended me to Ted. Tom had played for Arsenal and England in his younger days and I still chuckle when I remember him sitting on our sofa, flashing his medals, trying to persuade my parents that I, too, could have a collection like that one day. Those medals certainly impressed my dad, who was an old army man. But what impressed me most about Southampton was their uniquely gifted England international winger, Terry Paine. I drooled over him at every Saints home match I saw as a boy. And the thought of getting on the end of his crosses had me trembling with anticipation even then."

As it turned out, brash young Mick did not have long to wait to turn that dream into reality. He became the youngest-ever player to turn out for Southampton reserves when he was just 15 and a year later he was in the same first-team as Paine.

CHAPTER SEVEN

ALE HOUSE FOOTBALLERS

The first lesson that the young Mick Channon learned about becoming a professional footballer in the 1960s was that if you wanted to survive in the jungle that was the dressing room you had to develop the necessary social skills to enable you to succeed as a piss artist *par excellence*. As for the ball artist bit, well, that came naturally to him.

The shock of switching so rapidly from school milk to milk stout still remains with him till this day. "I just couldn't believe how many of the first team used to turn up for training nursing hangovers," he recalls. "Nor what bullies so many of those old arses were towards us kids. I now know that it was all part of the tradition of the game and that the morning after the night before can make grumpy old gits of us all. Cleaning their boots was bad enough, but when it came to clearing up their sweaty socks and jockstraps, pinching your nose was as important as buttoning your lip and God help you if you didn't knock on the door first before you went into their dressing room."

The mature Mick has since socialised with some of racing's hunting, shooting and fishing types, of course, and over a tincture or two has heard their horror stories of fagging for their seniors at public school. "But they had it easy compared to us apprentices," he insists. He was not alone in his amazed reaction to encountering this incredible hard-drinking culture, which was certainly not confined to the playing ranks. As a young football reporter based in Birmingham a few years earlier, I had been astonished to discover that the hospitality at many of the Midlands clubs was so warm and lavish that after midweek evening matches most of us scribes were not expected to crawl out of the various boardrooms and managers' and secretaries' offices until well into the wee small hours.

This free drinking became such a major part of our lives that on match days and nights the press corps would, more often than not, share a couple of cars and appoint one of our number as the non-drinking driver of each vehicle. Compared to us, Mick and his mates had it easy. At least they could sweat the booze out of their systems on the training ground. All we had available as a restorative was a hair of the dog. Although he was not to know it when he first signed for Southampton, Channon was entering a veritable academy in the art of getting rat-arsed. So much so that his beloved Saints were destined to be christened "The Ale House Brawlers" by legendary Liverpool manager Bill Shankly. All this time later he confesses: "Dear old Bill's nickname had such a nice homespun ring to it that most of us rascals did our worst to live down to it for years afterwards."

As for myself, many years later, after I had reached such a low point of my life that I was in danger of dying from alcoholism, I spent many agonising hours trying to analyse why drink and sport were such unlikely bedmates. Some of the reasons were glaringly obvious, of course, such as the bonhomie that men have always enjoyed through the medium of team games; the victory celebrations; the drowning of sorrows in defeat; the ultra-competitive nature of top sportsmen to outdo each other at anything and everything and, perhaps less recognisably but no less importantly, the amount of adrenaline that the excitement of sporting theatre manufactures. It was this excess of adrenaline-fuelled energy that we were all hooked on as much as the drink.

By the time Mick had made it into the Saints first-team, I had graduated to Fleet Street, which meant that I travelled with club and international sides when they played in Europe and beyond. So I not only saw their drunken antics at first hand but shared in them, too. This was long before the days when football became the new rock'n'roll and agents and assorted acolytes whisked the stars away to count their fortunes in a more salubrious world of expensive restaurants, fine wines and strict diets. Before that, soccer writers travelled on the same planes, trains and buses as the players and, as often as not, we slept in hotel rooms adjacent to them. Southampton happened to have even more excess boozing baggage in the shape of the then famous local pop group The Wurzels, who regaled their heroes with choruses of "Drink Up Thy Cider", a drunken ditty that they performed regularly on television.

The closest thing to a current superstar that Southampton football club could boast of possessing at that time was the aforementioned Terry Paine, who was a fringe member of Sir Alf Ramsey's 1966 World Cup-winning England squad and, incidentally, won all 19 of his international caps while the Saints were playing in the unfashionable Second Division – a feat that would be unimaginable today.

"Painey was the best player I ever played with or against," asserts Mick. "Ted Bates always said that the mark of a truly great pro was the number of years he managed to play after reaching

30." Paine certainly fitted that particular bill as he lasted 18 unbroken years with Southampton and clocked up a record 713 league games for the club. But Mick also acknowledges that Terry was regarded as a "little shit" by almost every opposition player with whom he ever came face to face – and he was called even worse than that by those who never saw him coming before he put the boot in. Mick still can't sing the man's praises highly enough as far as soccer skills and cunning are concerned. "At his best Terry had great pace and could beat four or five opponents with his trickery rather than his running. He was more of a jinker than a dribbler in the classic Sir Stanley Matthews manner. And even David Beckham has nothing on him when it comes to the age old art of crossing the ball," he purrs. But as a sly, foul tackler this slightly-built man with a sadistic streak running through him lived up to his name and was on practically every opposition player's personal hit list.

"They could never catch the dirty little sod, though," grins Mick. "He was far too crafty for that. As for me, I developed such a telepathic understanding with the man on the pitch that as soon as our eyes met in the opposition half I knew what he was going to do with the ball the moment he got possession of it. I scored hundreds of goals for Southampton just by catching a glance from Painey. Those eyes of his told me exactly what he was going to do but the defenders marking me didn't know so I could invariably steal that vital yard on them."

Apart from forming their mutual admiration society on matters of football, this odd couple were decidedly different in personality and outlook off the pitch. Typically of the happy-go-lucky character young Channon eventually became, it is not for some piece of footballing magic that he chooses to remember his old idol but instead for a hilarious cameo of Ale House tomfoolery. One of Mick's best mates then and now is Brian

O'Neil, a tough little midfielder who claimed he could feel no pain and appointed himself the new young star's minder on the field of play. According to Mick, O'Neil was such a quirky scatterbrain that he never wore the same pair of boots two games running. And this was a man who was good enough to play for England Under-23s, the Football League and to be on the fringe of Sir Alf Ramsey's all-conquering England squad.

"Brian was the only professional footballer I ever knew who never owned his own pair of boots," laughs Mick. "Every match day, you could find him rummaging around for some boots to nick and you had to have your wits about you to make sure he didn't pinch yours. Brian's drink in those days was vodka and water or 'vodka-agua' as he used to call it. And he could really lash it down." Never more so, apparently, than on a trip to Japan after the Saints had played a tour game in Kobe. During the post-match shenanigans, right-back Ken Jones foolishly challenged O'Neil to a one on one drinking contest. During the course of it, the pair stood eyeball to eyeball at the bar swallowing beer and vodka chasers in extremely rapid succession.

Mick takes up the commentary: "Ken, a no-nonsense Yorkshireman, proceeded to prove what most of us already knew – that he was in the Guinness Book of Records class when it came to supping ale. At about one in the morning, Ken swallowed the dregs of yet another drink while Brian had half a glass left. In the next moment Brian's drink had gone, but suddenly the floor beneath him was soaking wet. Ken went crazy, bellowing at Brian: 'You threw that on the floor, you cheating bastard.' This sparked off a row and the pair of them, both dead drunk, slowly shaped up to fight each other as the rest of us gathered round to watch the fun. Painey, always the first to see the worst side of any situation, started laughing himself silly and then he sniggered: 'Brian's pissed himself.' Sure enough, Brian's light grey trousers had turned a very dark colour indeed and this had the rest of us doubled up with laughter, too. But Brian happened to be Painey's room-mate on that trip and I soon wiped the smirk off his face when I announced: 'By the way, lads, Brian put Painey's trousers on to come out tonight!' The always immaculately dressed Terry had been undone by that habit Brian had of borrowing things. Getting back to those borrowed boots for a moment, Brian probably did have a pair issued by the club originally, but once they had worn out he obviously never bothered to get them replaced."

Southampton may have been a bit of a ragbag outfit back then but they were still good enough to qualify for Europe and the old Fairs Cup in 1969-70. For this, their first big foray into the big time, the Saints were drawn against a Portuguese team called Guimaraes, whose ground was situated north of Oporto, the city into which Southampton flew. The weather was scorching hot and the poor old Ale House lads' throats must have felt as dry as the Sahara desert. They could only look on in forlorn jealousy as the pressmen accompanying them on the lengthy journey north got stuck into the duty-free booze from the flight.

The return bus journey could not have been more different. I can only assume that the Saints' prowess as boozers had preceded them because before the kick-off of the game the Portuguese players presented every one of the Ale House 16-man squad with a bottle of vintage port – and the presentation took place on the pitch, of all places. The game was played in a new, half-built stadium where the visiting dressing room consisted of bare brick walls and little wooden chairs. To make it even worse, there had not been so much as a single bottle of Coke to quench those raging Ale House thirsts. There was, of course, only one solution – out came the presentation port – plus the extra bottles that had been given to the directors and the press. By the time they arrived back in Oporto everyone – players, press and directors, were all practically pie-eyed.

On another occasion, I remember accompanying those same Saints to Bilbao on a chartered propeller plane that broke down at the airport immediately before the return journey. Stuck there in the departure lounge for the best part of a day, there could only be one result – we all got as pissed as parrots. So much so that dear old Ted Bates, the manager, carted the players off to some nearby training ground to try and straighten them out a bit. And before he went, Bates turned to me and said: "As for you pressmen, you can run round and round the tarmac on the airport runway until we return." And he meant it.

For, believe it or not, in contrast to today's in-your-face 30-somethings, our generation were expected to respect elderly football managers. I remember that old Stan Cullis, the famous "Master of Molineux" in Wolverhampton Wanderers' heyday, used to take disciplinary measures so far that he would have us younger reporters standing to attention with the thumbs down the seams of our trousers, in the manner of army recruits, whilst he administered the mother and father of a bollocking to us whenever we upset him, which was often.

Teenaged Channon was only a few months older than Wayne Rooney, the current teenage boy wonder, was when Rooney made his debut for Everton. Channon's introduction to first-team football for Southampton came on Easter Monday 1966 and he scored against Bristol City on that first appearance to help the Saints into the First Division for the first time in their history. Channon had lost count of the number of goals he had scored before he left The Dell for the first time, 11 years after his baptism there. Unknown to him, he had hit 199. "If I'd been counting, I'd have stayed at the crease for my double century," he quips now.

Other memorable characters in that promotion-winning outfit included excellent players such as Ron Davies, Jimmy Melia, John Sydenham, Hughie Fisher, Dennis Hollywood and equally good players but even more world-class ravers like Jimmy Gabriel and John McGrath. Man-mountain McGrath was a colossus of a centre-half of the same size and stature as Bill Shankly's own favourite Ron Yeats. It would have needed a pneumatic road drill to damage those tree trunk-legs of his and it was undoubtedly big "Jake", as he was known to his team-mates, whom Shankly had most in mind when he conjured up that memorable "Ale House Brawlers" epithet. Sadly, after a brief spell in management, big John died of a heart attack a few years later.

Strangely for someone like Channon, who later in his England career professed to hate Scotland and the Scots, he formed some very close friendships with several Scottish club team-mates. First Jimmy Gabriel, then Asa Hartford at Manchester City and later Jim Steele in the Saints' FA Cup-winning team of 1976. He says of Scottish international Gabriel. "Apart from being a great drinking buddy, Jimmy was every inch a Scot – a stubborn devil – and I hated him at times. He always wanted to be the best and the only Englishman I know who was as intense about the game as 'Gabby' was Alan Ball."

Win, lose or draw on a Saturday, the Ale House lads made a ritual of their Sunday lunchtime session together in a local boozer where Jimmy Gabriel, who also wanted to be the best at drinking, would normally leave them all for dead when it came to raising his arm. "But one Sunday," Mick recalls, "Jim, who was getting on a bit then, shocked us all by announcing that he had to start losing weight and that after this particular session he was never going to touch another drop. He was as good as his word until the following Friday when he staggered into training absolutely reeking of booze. You couldn't get within ten yards of him and just tackling him would have been enough to get you breath-tested.

"We all demanded an explanation," laughs Mick, "and after training he told us: 'You won't believe this, but I was sitting on the sofa in front of the television last night, the missus had gone to bed and I was watching *The High Chaparral*. A cowboy has come into the bar and ordered up a bottle of whisky. It was slid down the bar to him, he put it to his lips and swallowed it all back, almost in one go. I just couldn't believe that was possible. So I got up, went to the drinks cabinet, lifted a bottle of Scotch – and I drank it! Being a perfectionist, I just wanted to see if it could be done. At the end of it, I was so legless that I just couldn't get out of the chair. I had to throw a shoe up at the ceiling to get the wife down to drag me up the stairs to bed.'

"Fortunately for Jimmy he must have had hollow legs because all that boozing never seemed to affect his later life. The last I heard of him was that he was coaching director of Washington University in America." Although he was not much more than a boy himself when he was thrown into the deep end with them, Mick still credits that bunch of blokes with providing him with the happiest days of his life. "They taught me as many bad habits as good ones but the best and most lasting lesson that I gleaned from them was how to enjoy life to the hilt and to get the very most entertainment out of every day. I remember the late, great Danny Blanchflower once saying that when you finish playing, the rest of your life is paying-up time. And if me and my old Ale House mates had to do it all again most of us would probably not change a thing."

CHAPTER EIGHT

HORSES

Ask Mick Channon for a tip on the gee-gees and he will reply instantly: "Never fall in love with one." For he has known some obsessive punters who have chased their losses on one particular flight of fancy right into the bankruptcy courts. Romances between humans and equines are, in his view, strictly for schoolgirls and show ponies and for his old mate and one-time neighbouring celebrity trainer, Jenny Pitman.

Yet he himself got hooked on horses as early in life as his teenage years, at around the same time as he was pulling on his first pair of football boots for money as a paid apprentice professional. Thoroughbred racehorses became as familiar a sight for him as his next-door neighbours for the simple reason that these fascinating animals walked through his village every day. An elderly trainer, by the wonderfully horsey-sounding name of Richmond Sturdy, stabled his small string just over the hill from the Channon household. Mick remembers him as a "stern old boy" who did not give the local lads a very warm welcome when he found them hanging around his stables most evenings.

All these years on, Mick is almost ashamed to confess that it was not only the horses who were grabbing his attention, but the stable lasses too. And he goes so far as to admit that it was one of these rosy-cheeked young maidens who eventually made him the man he is today. For not only did he get his first kiss and cuddle behind Mr Sturdy's stable but among the sweet nothings that the lass concerned whispered into his ear was a tip for the Ebor Handicap winner Tintagel II which became the subject of the first-ever Channon ante-post wager at 100 to 8, which then shrank to 6 to 1 when it became generally known that the maestro himself, Lester Piggott, was riding it. More significantly, at Sturdy's stable Mick's natural inquisitiveness was fed by knowledgeable answers from assistant trainers Paul Cole and Neville Callaghan, who were both to make progress towards becoming leading lights in the training ranks themselves. So just as so many young pro footballers from the inner cities whiled away their off-duty hours in snooker halls, the young Channon found himself becoming more and more familiar with horseboxes.

He may not have exactly fallen in love with the occupants of those boxes but he did, as a fellow athlete, come to respect and admire racehorses, both collectively and individually, the more he got to know about them. And the person mainly responsible for passing on this wisdom was a jockey named Frank Morby. "Now this was a man I came to love and respect almost as much as family," explains Mick. Along with the late Ted Bates at Southampton, Morby had more to do with fashioning Channon's incredible double sporting life than any other single individual. He describes Bates as a "tremendous character" who will always be "Mr Southampton in my eyes". Bates took the Saints from the Third to the First Division and laid the foundations for the stability they have enjoyed ever since. "I find it hard to put into words how much I owe to Ted for both the footballer and the man I became and I still count him as one of my oldest friends even if he did moan and groan that I ought to be tipping him winners every day."

Frank Morby was, in those days, a weather-beaten, leathery-faced veteran known in the business as a "chalk jockey". This was someone who did not get as many rides as the more illustrious members of the weighing room fraternity. He mostly rode the awkward squad, the cussed, crazy ones whom none of the big names fancied riding. For his sins, he also got the leg-up on the rank bad useless ones. But this ego-deflating experience did not, according to Channon, stop Frank from oozing an irrepressible enthusiasm for the racing game which rubbed off on his young, soccer-playing pal and stayed with Mick always. That chalk-jockey epithet was applied to Frank and other work riders like him because their names were hastily scribbled in chalk on the wall above their weighing room coat hangers. Back then, the Piggotts, the Scobie Breasleys, the Eph Smiths et al had their names beautifully inscribed on scrolls that could be rolled up and down rather like a church hymn list. But when the racetrack officials got down to the Frank Morbys and his ilk their claim to fame was to see their monikers – as often as not, misspelt – scrawled up on bare brick as "additional runners and riders."

"Not that I had it much better myself back then," recalls Mick. "As apprentices we were frightened to death to even go into the first-team dressing room. When we knocked on the door, the old arses inside knew we were nervous and played up to it. They never ever let you in without shouting through the door: 'What the fuck do you want?' And to eventually be given your own place beneath a coat hanger was the biggest of big deals – except that we had numbers not names."

Channon and Morby first met when Frank was work rider for Vernon Cross, who trained at Chattis Hill, which was just up the road from Mick's home village. At the same time he palled up with the now-legendary trainers Richard Hannon and David Elsworth, who were both a few years older than him. "Richard was assistant to his father, Harry; David was a bit lower down the pecking order in those days. He drove the horsebox for Vernon Cross. We were all country boys from the same part of the world and the more we got to know each other so we ganged up and drank together whenever we were off duty," says Mick.

They all climbed the racing ladder together, too. Frank later got himself a great job as work rider to Bernard Van Cutsem and he ended up in Kenya, where he became champion jockey. Back in those early days, however, Frank started getting more and more rides from various stables, mainly from Harry Hannon, and as Mick's enthusiasm grew he could not wait to finish training in the morning in time to drive Frank to the race meeting at which he was due to ride, whichever one it was. "I became Frank's unpaid chauffeur and loved every minute of it," says Mick. "As a young man I enjoyed a modest bet when we went racing, but the greatest thing Frank did for me was to introduce me to Newmarket and to so many of the horse-racing people who lived and worked there.

"For a working-class country lad like me, who by now had his head buried in breeding books, Newmarket was the academic equivalent of Oxbridge. The first time we drove into Six Mile Bottom was as exciting a journey for me as the ride up Wembley Way and the straight mile at Ascot were to become later in my life." But the young Mick was not really cut out to be a chauffeur – even an unpaid one. His daredevil driving style more often than not resulted in engines conking out on him in mid-journey rather like a steeplechaser having to be pulled up after taking too much punishment from the jockey's stick. "In fact, confesses Mick: "I was so flash then that as I put my foot down, I used to hang my right hand out of the window and pretend to whip my old motors up the hills no matter what the weather."

So it was fitting that his first encounter with David Elsworth was when, after his car had broken down on the way to the races one day, he flagged for a lift in a passing horsebox that was being driven by Elsworth for Vernon Cross, who recalls: "In those days Mick looked more like a rock star than an up-and-coming footballer, with his long hair, flared trousers and loud mouth. But he had an engaging personality that soon grew on you." And while Channon was growing on Elsworth, David himself was forging his own illustrious racing career that was to make him arguably the best dual-purpose trainer in the business. Later, he famously won the 1989 Gold Cup, the 1988 Whitbread, four King George Vl Chases and the Irish Grand National with the legendary Desert Orchid as well as the Grand National with Rhyme 'N' Reason. He also won the Champion Chase twice with Barnbrook Again and the Triumph Hurdle with Oh So Risky. And his successes on the Flat include the Irish 1,000 Guineas, the Coronation Cup, the Judmonte International and the Champion Stakes, all with In The Groove. He also won the Racing Post Trophy with Seattle Rhyme, the Ayr Gold Cup with Sarcita, the Cambridgeshire with Lear Spear and, more recently, a mountain of prize money with his current staying-race icon Persian Punch.

Of Channon, Elsworth says: "He had and still has a quick temper, he can be very aggressive, very determined and he is extremely energetic – all qualities which made him such a successful soccer star and just what the doctor ordered, too, as far as training goes. But the greatest thing Mick has going for him in his present profession is that he knows how to take it on the chin when he loses. He doesn't like losing but he takes it like a man.

"Mind you, even losing is probably becoming easier to live with for him now that he is training so many winners. Just to think that I used to train for him when he first became an owner and now we're rivals and he's leaving me in his slipstream. We might be the best of pals, but this is a tough business we're in and if I've got a serious horse that I think I might win with and he goes and beats me I'm not too pleased. But if anyone has to beat me, I'd rather it is Channon or Hannon. I'm not a bit surprised by his success, though. Years ago, when he was just starting out, we were having a few drinks together when I overheard him say to a mutual pal of ours: 'That fucking Elsworth might be a genius and all that, but I'm a grafter and I'll have him one day – just you wait.' But he wasn't being vindictive, he was just being Channon. And it looks like he's been proved right, doesn't it? I was really choked last season when I finished third in the 2,000 Guineas and he finished second, but if he had finished first and me second I think I'd have strangled him.

"Mind you, I think I frightened the life out of him at our local track, Salisbury, one day last season when I gave him a great big smacker on the cheek just like a footballer when his mate has scored the winning goal. I had been waiting for what seemed like an eternity for my 1,000th winner of my career, which is quite a feat for anyone. Our two horses were involved in a photo-finish for first place. When my filly got the verdict I turned and gave Mick a kiss and he looked astonished because he had forgotten all about me and my 1,000. The cheeky sod punished my amorous gesture, though, by making me buy the drinks instead of the other way around.

"Still it hasn't all been winners and kisses – far from it. Mick didn't just gatecrash into this game: he served a hard, self-imposed apprenticeship and I get the utmost pleasure from watching him grafting his way towards the champion trainer's title now. And so does our old mate Richard Hannon, although as a previous champion Hannon is still doing his best to stop Mick from overtaking him. As for me, it's great fun watching them battling away just so long as I continue to notch up the odd winner myself."

Richard Hannon is everything Mick still aspires to be – a former champion trainer, the Queen's trainer, a multi-Classic winner and, says Mick: "An all-round good old boy." Last season, however, the pupil turned master when, for the first time, Channon finished in front of his mate and mentor in the winners' table and Hannon had to pay for it in hard cash. "He owed me a monkey for the bet we had on who would train the most winners in the season and I couldn't wait to collect," grins Mick. Hannon smiles when reminded of this and says: "Sadly there was more punishment to come for my stable. My son and assistant, Richard, had a similar bet to me, only the stakes were a slap-up wine and dine job at one of those really posh joints. And I have to confess that I think most of our stable lads have a few small side bets with each other." Old master Richard beams with pride when he is reminded that Mick gives him and their joint pal, David Elsworth, the credit for teaching him most of what he knows about the training game.

"I suppose the main thing I taught him was that you have to have horses right across the board and that when you have them you run them," says Richard. "They are no good to you sitting in the stable. The point about having all types of horses in your yard is that when the entries turn up to be made you have horses for nearly every type of race. We buy cheap ones as well as expensive ones so that we are happy to run ours in auction plates and median auctions. A lot of races break up after the initial entries are made so we are always in with a shout. They say Mick and I have a lot of runners but the answer to that is that we have a lot of winners, too.

"I had 120 domestic winners last season and six overseas and I must say I didn't expect to see Mick come whooshing past me like he did with his 140 and several more abroad. It's the first time he's beaten me, so he's top of the tree, winner-wise. Let's hope he doesn't make too much of a habit of it, eh? Still, if I can't win, I'd rather see Mick do it than anyone else. Money-wise, though, it will always be hard for us to beat the likes of Sir Michael Stoute and Mark Johnston, who usually get the better horses sent to them."

CHAPTER NINE

SAINTS

Down at The Dell in the 1960s, young Mick Channon's star was rising season by season. While he was still a teenager, he scored eight goals in one season: 1967-68. The following season, 1968-69, he scored 12 more and, as if to mark his ascent into manhood, he notched up 21 in his 21st year in 1969-70. His playing style was 30 years before its time. In the days of tricky inside-forwards, dribbling wingers and battering-ram centre-forwards, Mick went at defenders from all angles. He was the fastest young-gun in the business – so much so that he could have beaten Linford Christie over the first ten yards. He was as dangerous coming from a wide position as he was cutting through the middle. Just as impressive was his consistency. His form never seemed to dip. His seasonal goals tallies from 1970 until he was transferred to Manchester City seven years later were 20, 17, 18, 23, 29, 25 and 25 again.

He had a variety of striking partners during that time and seasoned goalscorers such as Welsh international Ron Davies and

England stars Martin Chivers and Peter Osgood found themselves playing second fiddle to him. Naturally, there were comings and goings in most of the other positions at Southampton, too, but one thing never changed. "Every one of us was proud to be known as a traditional 'Ale House Brawler'," says Mick. One thing that worried the club's bosses was that when they tried to sign new recruits they often had to overcome the reluctance of some of them to join the club because they had heard the advice which spread round the game's dressing rooms. This was: "Whatever you do, don't sign for Southampton or the stench in the changing room will suffocate you." For the rumour was that Mick Channon and his racing buddy Brian O'Neil came in for training every day reeking of horse shit after they had mucked out their horseboxes earlier in the morning.

Perhaps more importantly, from Southampton's point of view, Channon also turned out to be something of a lucky charm for the club. His first spell there coincided with the Saints' first-ever spell in the top flight – eight years of it. And he was also elevated to club captain. The Saints were relegated in 1975 but the biggest event in their history was still to come when, as a Second Division club, they defeated Manchester United 1-0 in the 1976 FA Cup final at Wembley.

Like hundreds of other Cup finalists before and after him, Mick's memories of the events of that match are strictly limited. Most of it flew past in a blur of adrenaline-fuelled excitement. One scene is forever etched like a still photograph in his mind, however, and that is the sight of Bobby Stokes scoring the winner for Saints. Stokes later died of pneumonia at the tragically young age of 44. "And if ever that famous old phrase 'only the good die young' applied to anyone it applied to Bobby," says Mick. "He looked like a fresh-faced choirboy and was loved by absolutely everyone who came into contact with him."

Mick recalls most of the events before and after the big game vividly and none more so than the bizarre way in which he celebrated the event. As the Saints' post-match banquet became ever livelier, Mick departed with his first wife Jane and mother, Betty. He left his team-mates in their revelry to go and gaze in awe at the birth of the first foal he ever owned and which he named Royale Final. She never managed to win a race herself, but she did eventually give birth to a great jumper called Ghofar who won the Hennessy Gold Cup. And to add even more spice to that story, Royal Final was the direct result of what in these more cynical times would be described as a "bung".

Her mother, Blur Horizon, was one of two horses given as a gift to Channon from the then president of Southampton Football Club, Herbert Blagrave. Mick remembers: "I was old Herbert's blue-eyed boy at the time and on top of that I had just asked for a transfer and he wanted to keep me. So, knowing that I was mad-keen on horses, he decided to give me a couple of broodmares.

"Royal Final was born at Jamesmead, the little stud farm I had bought by then. My brother, Phil, had been looking after the shop and he suddenly phoned and said: 'Never mind a little thing like a Cup Final, get your arse down here to watch this beautiful birth.'"

Channon's hands should have been the ones wrapped around that 1976 FA Cup when it was first raised aloft at Wembley but in asking for a transfer he had also reluctantly forsaken the captaincy. "The reason I wanted to move was the same one that still bothers relegated players today. I was an England regular and did not want Second Division football to rust my form for international matches," he explains. "I was happy for full-back Peter Rodrigues when he got the job and consoled myself that our '76 team was chock-full of captains anyway. Ossie, Jim Steele and Jim McCalliog, for instance, were always nagging the rest of the lads. I think it was the old arses like them that helped us to shock United, who were packed with so many of the bright young things of their day." There is another ironic little twist to that Cup-final story in that it was the last time the Queen ever presented the trophy and in view of her later connection with Channon it would have been even more apt if it had been him collecting the cup on behalf of his team.

But Mick's other less pleasant memory of the events surrounding that magical occasion was his part in the perennial scandal of the sale of black market tickets. For, like almost every other player in living memory at that time, Channon handed over Cup Final tickets that he knew would end up in the hands of the ticket touts. No issue in football ever got more people worked up into a rage than the selling of Cup-final tickets by the participating players. And when Southampton's turn came to tread the lush, green turf of Wembley, they were no exception to the rule in the annual ritual of making some people pay over the odds for the privilege of watching them do it.

Today, Channon says that he can understand and sympathise with the fans who could not get a precious ticket and could not afford the black market price. But even though this naturally generous man still feels pangs of guilt about his part in this dodgy practice, he maintains that in those days of relatively poorly paid players, most of whom only got one chance in a lifetime to make a few extra quid out of entertaining millions, their actions were justified in this less than pure pursuit of perks. "The glory of appearing in a Cup final gave you a great feeling," he says. "But remember most of us lads regarded ourselves as tradesmen not celebrities and, right or wrong, money seemed to be the only means we had of measuring our worth back then."

He adds: "I would be a liar if I claimed I had never sold a black market ticket and so would every other player I knew back then.

The feelings about building a nest egg for when your playing days were over were intense for all of us."

So unless you happen to be a paragon of virtue, someone who has never fiddled their expenses, never told white lies over money matters and do not have a hypocritical bone in your body I advise you to discontinue reading the rest of this less than puritanical page. For I couldn't help chuckling when several years after that final I was sent by my newspaper to interview Southampton manager Lawrie McMenemy in Malaysia to find out if he was about to accept Manchester United's reported offer of their manager's job and, if so, to offer him a princely payment for a regular column. The first people I saw when I arrived at the Saints' hotel were Channon and his close mates, Alan Ball and Kevin Keegan, who were frolicking in the swimming pool at the time. I told them the biggest titbit of current esoteric news back home was that Fat Stan Flashman, the king of the ticket touts, had been robbed of hundreds of black market tickets at gunpoint. Their instant collective reaction was to laugh and then for Bally to exclaim: "Hope our names weren't printed on the back of 'em."

But it had been no laughing matter to Channon when he learned that his own testimonial match on the Monday evening following the final had also fallen into the clutches of the ticket touts. He says: "My testimonial match had been fixed up long in advance but it just happened that we had won the Cup on the previous Saturday. It was almost embarrassing for me, really, because they were queueing for tickets at six o'clock on Monday morning and that was a situation absolutely unheard of for a testimonial game. Tickets had been on sale for months past, but by eleven o'clock on the morning of the match they had all gone."

The pandemonium wasn't just to pay tribute to Mick Channon, of course, popular as he was at The Dell. The reason the ground was packed to the rafters was that all the local fans wanted to see the Cup paraded again so that they could relive the one and only day their club had ever won the FA Cup.

"I'll always remember walking into the ground that night and seeing the players of Queens Park Rangers, who were the opposition, handing their tickets through the coach window to the touts," Mick remembers. "It suddenly hit me just what a massive event this was turning into and I squirmed as some season-ticket holders yelled at me that they hadn't even got tickets for it. I thought to myself: 'I'm probably the only player in history who has had tickets for his testimonial sold on the black market.

"Financially it could not have worked out better. The official attendance was 29,000 and the receipts were £23,000. It beggars belief, of course, how big that amount would have been now, almost 30 years later. The reason I had the testimonial was that I'd been with the Saints since I was a kid – I'd never had a move then or any other sort of lump sum payment – it was a reward for ten years of loyal service. I can assure you that by the time I got my hands on what was left of the cash after tax and expenses it was no big total but I had no complaints at all because I was being paid for something I loved doing anyway. And it turned out to be the perfect way for those lucky enough to get into the ground to celebrate winning the Cup."

Incidentally, as a postscript to this, the perennial dodgy tickets saga, I defy anyone to beat this for black humour. When West Bromwich Albion played Everton in the Cup Final of 1968, I was based in the Midlands for the *Sunday People* so I accompanied the Albion party to their celebration banquet and beyond after which most of us wound up in the swanky Astor Club in Mayfair, courtesy of my gangster brother, Jim, who did a bit of unofficial minding there in those days. Well, I happened to know beyond dispute that "Sulky", the club's well-known master of ceremonies in those days' had helped the players to dispose of their surplus tickets on the black market and then had the nerve to turn some of them away at the door when they arrived in the wee small hours because he said he was full up.

CHAPTER TEN

FINAL

The fact that he recalls more about the birth of his filly than the 1976 Cup final itself is the biggest clue as to what really makes Mick Channon tick. Despite making himself such a distinctive figure as a striker, horses will always take precedence over football in Mick's psyche because his soccer skills were an inborn gift from the gods whilst racing was his man-made obsession. As a football personality, he will always be remembered for the one-armed, whirling-windmill gesture he made in celebration of his goals. Peter Osgood, incidentally, reckons that Mick stole that trademark from Pete Townshend of The Who. I will have to take his word for that because, as a dinosaur member of the Al Jolson and Frank Sinatra fan clubs, I can't recall seeing Pete and his musical mates in action. I suspect, though, that Mick's brother, Phil, is nearer the mark when he chuckles: "The reason for Mick swinging his arm that way was simply because he was never fit enough to be able to do somersaults like Robbie Keane."

So extraordinarily gifted was Mick as an athlete that he barely needed to concentrate too hard on honing his rare talent for the game of football. The lifelong indulgence of his horses hobby, however, took up endless hours of study. Like most other working people, Channon needed a hobby, or in his case a passion, to take their minds off the day-to-day routine of earning the daily bread, no matter how glamorously that bread happened to be packaged. It meant that he became so absorbed in breeding books and form lines that, without being necessarily conscious of it, he barely had time to think about football. So much so that when his hobby turned into a living, he became an out-and-out workaholic. He gets up earlier in the mornings now than he often rolled home after a night out in the old days.

Maybe he is subconsciously driven by the early memories of the irreplaceable loss of his brother or by haunting memories of his nightmare days and nights on the scrapheap which he graphically calls the "glass mountain".

Ossie gives us a massive clue when he says: "I sometimes used to look at Mick during a match and watch him laughing and muttering to himself. I'm sure he was slightly mad. Unless he was thinking about how his horse was getting on in the 3.30." Someone who could back up that last point of view with cast-iron certainty was the late, great, television soccer commentator Brian Moore, who once told me that Mick had worked out an elaborate tic-tac system for Brian to provide him with the finishing order in a particular race with hand signals from his place on the gantry during the course of a game.

Osgood takes up the Cup Final story with this particular Channon gem, which sparked off the build-up to the big day. "The week after we beat Crystal Palace 2-0 at Stamford Bridge in the semi-final, we played up at Grimsby in a pedestrian Second Division league game. What made this trip different from the norm, though, was the fact that thousands of Saints fans had decided to make the long trip in order to salute us for reaching the final for them.

"On the Friday night before the game, Mick, who was a Southampton fan himself, of course, invited all the players to his hotel room and announced: 'This is the proudest moment in my football career and I think we should all be celebrating big time – so the drinks are on me.'

"None of us were proud of it, but we all staggered out of Mick's room at five o'clock on the morning of the match legless – the lot of us. The rumpus from the room must have reached Lawrie's ears at some stage and understandably he was furious. As we sat in the dressing room, nursing our sore heads, his pre-match talk went something like this: 'You lads should be thoroughly ashamed of yourselves. There are thousands of fans out there who've travelled half of the country today. And do you know why? Because they are so fucking proud of you, that's why. Shame on the lot of you.'

"Lawrie certainly succeeded in making us feel ashamed but physically we couldn't raise ourselves to play in the first half. There were more backpasses and sideways balls than there were in the entire season. We were dead lucky to traipse in at half time with the score at 0-0. The big man's temper had not improved. He ripped into us again: 'I can't even look at you, I'm not even sure that I want to be your manager any more.' But Mick, ever the optimist, suddenly pipes up: 'Don't worry, gaffer, we'll put it right this half.' He could say that again because he did no more than go out and score four goals in the second half himself and, with Bobby Stokes chipping in with another, we finished up winning 5-0.

"Afterwards, Lawrie didn't know whether to laugh or cry. All he could do was keep repeating: 'You lucky bastards. You lucky, lucky bastards.' And as Mick always likes the last word in an argument, he got that this time, too, when he cracked back at McMenemy: 'If the lager hadn't run out at 5am we'd have won 9-0.' "

Ossie also recalls that early in his time at Southampton he decided to tackle verbally Channon about his selfish style of play. "How come you hardly ever pass to me, Mick?" says Ossie. "Sorry, mate," says Mick. "I just can't help myself. The instant I see the whites of those posts I just have to go for goal." How ironic, then, that a few years later, when he had a torrid time as a Manchester City player, Mick claimed that one of the main reasons for his dip in form was the fact that City wingers Peter Barnes and Dennis Tueart preferred doing their party pieces by trying to take the lace out of the ball rather than passing it to him to put it in the net. But that's goalscorers for you – both Mick and Ossie were paid to be selfish about finding the net and to moan their heads off about it when they didn't.

Osgood also provides another massive insight into why so many of the stars of the 1970s were scallywags and rascals. Sir Alf Ramsey called him off the subs' bench to play for England in the 1970 World Cup and as he waited on the touchline to get on the pitch some of the other subs claimed they heard him turn his head back to them and growl: "Well at least I'll get my appearance money, boys." What he should and would have said if he had been totally true to himself was that he was tingling with anticipation, filled with excitement and had butterflies marauding around in his stomach. But the handicap that Ossie and Channon and most of their contemporaries suffered from was peer pressure. If you wanted to enjoy a good relationship with your pals in the dressing room you had to adopt the macho poses and attitudes that have always predominated when a group of like-minded guys get together. Even if they had wanted to behave like role models for the kids or choirboys for the mums, they didn't dare because their mates would have taken the piss out of them mercilessly.

And I must confess that I had a similar false mask on most of the time when I was masquerading as some kind of a cowboy with the rest of my press mates. Ossie also holds his hands up about flogging Cup-final tickets by offering the admission that most of the lads like him and Mick lived entirely in the moment and were almost always totally self-centred. "Our trouble was that we reached our lifetime's earning peak at a time when most of us had no inkling of what a lifetime was going to amount to. We were reckless with our money, our love and our futures," he says fatalistically.

It was in, a way, even more ironic, then, that the late and much-lamented Bobby Stokes, a modest local boy who made good locally, should score the only goal of such a star-studded final. And in truth, from the purist's point of view, Stokes's goal was one of the very few highlights of a cat-and-mouse-style encounter that never caught fire as a spectacle. And it was mostly down to the fact that the mice won it that it got such a prominent place in the annals of FA Cup history.

Laughing at more memories of that magical night after winning the Cup, Channon says: "When it came to wacky Ale House behaviour, I have to admit that my old strike partner, Peter Osgood, ran me close by nicking the cup and taking it home with him. And he even finished up in the early hours of the morning flashing it at a tea stall before eventually bringing it back safe and sound to The Dell." As a postscript, Ossie has one more memory jogger for his old pal Mick to ponder on when he says: "The silly old sod has got it all wrong about me nicking the cup on the night of the final. In fact, I pinched it a few weeks later when the team were guests of honour at the Tiberius gambling club in Southampton. The FA Cup was on display and as the drink flowed down me a prank started to form in my mind. And I bet a couple of the lads that I could nick the cup and get it out of the building. As it turned out I've never won a bet so embarrassingly easily. After the dinner had finished, I simply slipped back through a side entrance into the closed club, sought out the security man, gave him a cock and bull story about having some photos done with it and said I would bring it back as soon as the photo shoot was finished.

"Once I got it back outside I simply showed it off to Jim Steele and David Peach and then bundled it unceremoniously into the boot of the car. It was still only just chucking out time in the pubs so I drove into the city centre to show it off again. We stopped at a mobile burger van for a coffee and hot dog and before we knew it a boisterous crowd had descended upon us. Full of bravado, big, bad Jim Steele suddenly shouts to the crowd: 'Hang on, lads, we've brought you a little present.' So out of the boot comes the precious trophy, up go the cheers and into the cup pours everyone's tea and coffee so that we can all have a communal drink out of it.

"After that the three of us went on somewhere for a few more bevvies so you can just imagine how I felt when I opened my eyes to a desperate hangover next morning and there on the sideboard next to my car keys, my loose change and a few crumpled fivers stood the gleaming FA Cup. As Mick says, I did get it back to The Dell safe and sound eventually. But it was really a case of better late than never. And I suppose that just about sums up the twilight of my career with Mick and the other Ale House Lads at the dear old Dell."

CHAPTER ELEVEN
CATHY JANE

It was in the early 1970s that Mick Channon bought his first racehorse. The only other material possession that the then 22-year-old Channon owned was an Austin A35 motor car. Everyone around him was advising this rising young star to go for bricks and mortar as security against the wilderness years that inevitably followed most young professional soccer players' careers in those days. But by then he was so enamoured of the racing game that he knew he could not look forward to the rest of his life without the thrill of going to a racetrack whenever the opportunity arose.

In common with every other punter before him, he also burned his fingers enough times on the so-called good things he was being tipped that he realised the hard way that betting was not the answer to a life of fulfilment even though it could and would be almost as thrilling as winning a football match if it were kept in proportion. So the wise old head that had always paradoxically seemed fitted to those reckless young shoulders decided that owning and breeding was going to be the way forward for him. As for training, that was such an unlikely prospect that it was not even a gleam in his eye at that time.

Mick's racing sidekick, Frank Morby, marked his card that an ex-window cleaner named Ken Payne, who had started training at West Wellow, near Southampton, had some fair yearlings in his possession. Payne, incidentally, won a short-lived notoriety as "king of the selling races" with a series of well-publicised coups before his star eventually waned. So Mick persuaded his soccer sidekick, Brian O'Neil, to go halves with him on one of them. Before doing the deal, the well-informed Mr Channon already knew what Payne had paid for the animals at the Newmarket Sales so there was no chance of them being sold a pup.

Mick chose a filly that he and O'Neil agreed to name after their wives Cathy O'Neil and Jane Channon. He jokes now: "The idea behind that was to stop them nagging if they thought we were betting the housekeeping money on her." The fearless pair of Ale House lads paid £200 each for Cathy Jane and she changed Mick's life so completely that he says: "Everything I went on to achieve in racing was down to her, though after winning some serious races and giving birth to a string of winners herself, she eventually turned into as grouchy an old cow as you're ever likely to clap eyes on. She was so moody that before she finally went off to graze in that great lush meadow in the sky, she left me something very personal to remember her by in the shape of an ugly life-long scar on my upper-left arm where she took a lump out of it one of her bad hair days," adds Mick.

On purchasing Cathy Jane, Channon and O'Neil sent her to another local man, Bill Wightman, a much-respected, old-school trainer and a Second World War fighter pilot, who became yet another teacher from whom the ever-enthusiastic, horse-loving Mick could learn. Brian O'Neil did not sustain the interest or the enthusiasm to make racing his future life's work but he and Mick have stayed close ever since and are still in touch on a daily basis. They also shared some unforgettable racing days together, courtesy of Cathy Jane, although the little filly made them sweat and suffer for a long time before she surpassed their wildest dreams for her. As a two-year-old she turned out to be so backward that she not only never won a race, she embarrassed her jockey Frank Morby into admitting to Mick that she wasn't up to much. Mick recalls: "She was proving more expensive to run than my old motor and Brian and I found ourselves without two bob to rub together."

Cathy Jane proved so disappointing to Mick and his mate, Brian, that they were both ready to sell her and cut their losses. The problem was that by the time they reluctantly reached that decision all the sales were over and they were lumbered with the filly for another year. Then, as so often happens in tales of the turf, their world suddenly turned upside down. For although Bill Wightman agreed to put her into the Ascot sales when she reached three, he asked the Ale House lads if they minded him entering her in the odd race before she came under the hammer.

An added problem was that between them they did not know what the filly's best distance was. She had been useless as a two-year-old sprinter and not much better as a middle-distance horse. But a month before the sales Bill, more in desperation than hope, switched her from a mile and a quarter to two miles and she ran an absolute blinder to finish fourth at Wolverhampton against some very decent animals.

So it was a last-chance-saloon scenario when Mick, Brian and another Southampton team-mate, wild man Jim Steele, journeyed to Bath where, going for broke, Bill Wightman booked that peerless stylist Joe Mercer, who was the 'guvnor' at that course at that time, to ride her in a '13-furlong' race. And, hey presto, Cathy Jane found her optimum distance and so decided Channon's destiny. He recalls that he bet £3 on her to win at

7 to 1. Brian did not have a bet and disloyal Jim backed another horse in the same race, called Eleanor Queen. Then, in Brian's own words: "As they came towards the finish, out of a dog-leg, three-quarters-of-a-furlong out, Eleanor Queen was on the rails and coming up to challenge Cathy Jane who, would you believe it, was in the lead. The favourite, Oyster Bar, was on the outside when suddenly Oyster Bar veered right across the course, bumping into our horse and forcing us into Eleanor Queen just after we'd got the better of her.

"I had, of course, been roaring home Cathy Jane in the stands but the screams stuck in my throat as we crossed the line second. As soon as we got to the unsaddling enclosure Joe Mercer advised us to lodge an objection and told us we would definitely be awarded the race. At this point, we couldn't see Jim Steele's arse for dust as he legged it down to the bookies to bet on the objection verdict."

That decision went in Cathy Jane's favour so there could not have been a more dramatic way for an owner to register his first winner than this. More importantly, Cathy Jane proved to be such a stout stayer that she went on to win four important races in that category. When she won at glorious Goodwood, Mick had to use all his fame and charm to talk his way into the owners' and trainers' enclosure because he was most improperly dressed.

He recalls: "Lawrie McMenemy had only just joined Southampton as manager and, as is the way of new brooms, was making us train in the afternoons. I explained to him that I had a horse running this particular afternoon and needed to get to the races. Probably because I was the blue-eyed boy, I was excused training but Brian, who was never quite so fanatical about the gee-gees as I was, decided not to push his luck. "I turned up at Goodwood wearing jeans and a tee shirt which caused me to get more black looks than congratulatory handshakes from my fellow owners."

Cathy Jane's day of days came, however, when she won the prestigious Brown Jack Stakes at Ascot in the summer of 1973. The Brown Jack was one of the longest staying-races in the calendar but Mick remembers: "I don't know who was more knackered afterwards – her, her jockey, Willie Carson, or Brian and me. "It was during pre-season training at Southampton and we had been sent on a ten-mile, cross-country run that morning. Both Brian and I had enjoyed good nights out the previous evening so we were well and truly tailed off at the back.

"We must have looked like death warmed up by the time we got to the course because the first thing Willie said to us in the paddock was: 'Blimey, you two lads look a bit rough.' I retorted: 'If you'd worked as hard as we have this morning, Willie, you'd look rough, too.' This was a season when Willie was to become champion jockey, so you can understand my amazement and embarrassment when Brian got it into his head to issue the wee man with riding instructions. They went like this: 'Now, remember Willie, you just pretend to be the cowboy and let the rest of them be the Indians chasing you!'

"Obviously, Willie cocked a deaf 'un at Brian but he certainly rode like a demented cowboy, anyway. In his typical fashion, he pushed and scrubbed our filly from fully a mile out to win by a head on the line from a horse called Cumbernauld, which was ridden by Tony Murray, who was, tragically, much later in life to commit suicide. "I've still got photographs of the weals on Cathy Jane's rump from Willie's whip and as for Willie himself, as he rolled off her, he snarled: "Don't ever tell me about being knackered again. This was the hardest race I've had in my life.' "

Cathy Jane was to go on to become the catalyst for Mick's success as a breeder. In addition to his West Ilsley stable, he now owns and runs a 120-acre stud in West Tytherley, Wiltshire. At the time of Cathy Jane's success as a four-year-old, he thought he would never be able to afford to buy another horse so he decided to breed from her because she had been quite well bred herself on her dam's side and was by an Italian Derby winner, Lauso.

The rest, as they say, is history. He sent Cathy Jane to a decent little seven-furlong handicapper, Mandamus, and from him she produced what was to become Mick's next favourite horse: Man On The Run. "He wasn't a particularly good-looking colt, but he was a tough little bugger, just like his mum," says Mick. Man On The Run eventually won six races – three on the Flat and three over jumps – and was placed on more than 20 occasions. Another one of Cathy Jane's sons was Jamesmead, who not only finished second in the Cesarewitch, but actually won the Tote Gold Trophy.

Mick fondly remembers: "When Cathy Jane became a brood mare she was even more bitchy and moody than she had been as a racehorse. In all, she had seven foals and every one of them was a colt. That, of course, meant that I never had a filly to go on breeding from her.

"Her seven boys all turned out to be winners, but they were the end of the line – before she fractured a leg and had to be put down. But for the £400 she cost me and Brian she turned out to be worth her weight in gold both financially and, even more importantly, in the amount of pleasure and satisfaction she gave us." Before winding up the reminiscences on his beloved Cathy Jane, Mick records one last anecdote about her when he says: "One day, as usual, I was shouting and roaring my head off in the stands during one of her son's races. So much so that afterwards Bill Wightman advised me to become a manager when I finished playing. He said sarcastically: 'Michael, I've discovered something about your horses today – they love being shouted at just like you footballers do.'"

CHAPTER TWELVE

BIG LAWRIE

Back on the football front, Southampton and Channon, in particular, continued to imitate life itself by being in an almost constant state of flux. The only thing that time and circumstances did not alter was the mentality and behaviour of the hard core of experienced players – or the "old arses" as Mick also calls them. For, once an "Ale House Lad" always an "Ale House Lad" it seemed. Whilst Mick was winning England Under-23 caps and then graduating to Sir Alf Ramsey's full international squad in October 1972, like was being replaced by like on the playing front.

Mick succeeded Ron Davies as the main goal-getter. No slouch in the air himself, Channon still maintains that Davies was the best header of a ball he has ever seen. And no less a judge than Sir Matt Busby also went on record as declaring that Davies was the best centre-forward in Europe in his time. Welsh international Ron was also a talented enough cartoonist to have his work published in newspapers. Mick's favourite Davies drawing, incidentally, features his mate and co-racehorse owner Brian O'Neil and the then Saints coach, John Mortimore, who happened to be the possessor of a very large nose, shaped much along the lines of current Liverpool assistant-manager Phil Thompson's famous hooter. The Southampton gym had an asbestos roof and Mortimore would worry about the ball damaging it during training so he issued strict instructions that the ball was to be kept below head-height. But the Ale House Lads, and tough nut O'Neil in particular, were not having any of that. "In five-a-side matches in the gym it was every man for himself and there were some right battles," recalls Mick.

One day Brian lashed a shot straight into the roof and a tile came tumbling down, almost decapitating the coach in the process. Mortimore gave O'Neil a severe rollicking and in return he was later shown a cartoon from Ron Davies which depicted little Brian belting the ball up John's enormous nostril. This, of course, was immediately seized on by the rest of the team and pinned up on the dressing-room wall for posterity.

The Ale House Lads even found that like replaced like when the brilliant but ageing Scottish wing-half and ex-Everton star, Jimmy Gabriel, was succeeded by an even more notorious drinker in fellow Scot Jim Steele. Local legend has it that Steele wrote off more cars per season than they do on the Formula 1 Grand Prix circuit. And Jim was also to achieve another feat that should have got him into the Guinness Book of Records. For, according to Channon, this big defender became the all-time drinking star of the Saints' formidable array of Ale House tipplers. He clinched that title at a darts match of all things. Saints being such sinners when it came to boozing, they naturally had a darts team. One night, at a pub where most of them enjoyed a few after-hours pints, they played until around 11.30pm before heading for home. Mick remembers: "As usual, Steeley was the last to leave and as he lived in a pub, anyway, which just happened to be within walking distance of the one we were in, no one thought he was in any danger – until the next morning when he came in for training cut to pieces. He had, apparently, foolishly decided to go home in his old Jaguar and had gone straight through a roundabout before turning the Jag over and had been thrown through the windscreen. He had lain in the road unconscious with the car upside down and people from a nearby house had come out and covered him over with a blanket, thinking he was dead.

"He was rushed to hospital but the police couldn't breathalyse him because he was still unconscious. The next morning he woke up in the hospital, discharged himself and cadged a lift to get into training on time. Amazingly there was nothing seriously wrong with him physically, apart from all his cuts and bruises. After he eventually finished playing in America, big Jim worked in a liquor store over there. The last I heard of him he was, appropriately enough, running a pub in the Cotswolds."

But the biggest shock of all to the old Ale House way of life had come at the end of 1973 when Ted Bates, who was nearing retirement age, was promoted to the board of directors, to be replaced by Lawrie McMenemy.

By then, big Lawrie had achieved the seemingly impossible in generating a lot of publicity for his previous club, lowly, unfashionable Grimsby Town, where he attracted attention from the press with his commanding but courteous ex-guardsman demeanour and his articulate way with words. McMenemy was destined to enjoy unparalleled success with Southampton during his long reign at The Dell, during which he took the club decidedly up-market, chiefly by signing some of the biggest names in English football.

The most accurate description of Lawrie's unusual talents is, for me, provided by Mick Channon himself. He says: "Lawrie had this gift of taking experienced players and squeezing them like an orange, still managing to find some juice in the old arses even after they should have dried up. He knew that older, better players retained their form on a fairly regular basis and consequently made a team tick while youngsters tend to have emotional highs and lows and more frequent dips in form. And I have to admit that it's not all that different with racehorses, either.

"He was a good listener and he got something out of each player who passed through his hands – young or old. But he used to rule by fear with the kids, who were frightened to death of him. They had to be in for training by nine o'clock and were fined if they were late. He made regular checks at their digs to make sure they did not go astray there either. It was real army-style discipline that he obviously brought with him from his previous life in the military. The baths had to be sparkling, the showers immaculately clean and the toilets spotless." McMenemy also introduced a dress code that did not meet with Mick's approval. He did not like to see players wear jeans or appear at training unshaven. The headstrong young Channon often fell out with his new boss over this and plenty of other issues. But, older and wiser now, he says: "I have to admit that I can be a strict disciplinarian with the young work riders at my stable. I don't allow smoking or really slovenly attitudes."

Mick reckons that McMenemy took a long time to bury the bitterness he felt over the title Southampton gave him at first. He was officially described as manager designate as he served what appeared to be a trial period to prepare for his predecessor's retirement. "That tag used to irritate the hell out of Lawrie and so did my own idol, little Terry Paine," explains Mick. "The pair of them simply couldn't stand the sight of each other. They both had dominating personalities and both wanted to be top man. And it was no coincidence that Terry was ousted the moment old Ted went 'upstairs'. A similar situation arose much later with Lawrie and Kevin Keegan during my second spell with the Saints. They are both very strong characters. I can be a forceful type, too, but I never wanted to run the club." No wonder: for he had witnessed at first hand McMenemy begin his Southampton career by getting left at the starting gate and seeing his team relegated to the Second Division in 1974. He did not get them back up to the top flight again until four years later although he did manage to squeeze that history-making FA Cup-final victory into the equation in 1976.

Most of this coincided with what now fills Channon with shame. He was already an England superstar by then and now honestly admits: "There was a period at The Dell when I thought I was above everybody else there. Saying it to you now makes me hate myself. I thought I was Southampton and that if Mick Channon left the club it would fold up without him." Thankfully, some much-needed ego deflation was to be provided from a most unlikely source. It came via ex-Chelsea superstar Peter Osgood, who was the first of the string of really big-name signings on which Lawrie prided himself.

Osgood had a reputation as a playboy when he arrived and had lost a lot of the speed of movement and thought that had once made him such a joy to watch. That catalytic moment between he and Channon came during training one morning at around the time when once-proud Ossie denigrated himself in an interview with me by declaring that he had become Mick Channon's labourer at Southampton. He was also to become a life-long pal of Mick's and is still on the phone to him at West Ilsley almost every day. Mick remembers the incident in question this way: "I went into work one morning feeling out of sorts and not wanting to train. I hardly bothered to do a stroke of work and was obviously messing the whole thing up for everyone else.

Happy-go-lucky Ossie always gave the impression of strolling through life with a smile on his face so he was the last one I thought would have complained about my behaviour. But he suddenly rounded on me and roared: 'I've come all the way from Windsor to train. If you don't want to bother yourself, fuck off out of it!' At first, I was furious at his outburst, but the more I thought about it, the more I realised what a big-headed git I had become and vowed to change my ways. The last thing I wanted to do was to fall out with any of my Ale House mates."

It is proving hard to keep Osgood out of the Channon story. For although most contemporaries of this pair would point to Channon, Ball and Keegan as being the three inseparable musketeers, Ossie keeps shoulder-charging his way into these tales by the sheer force of his charismatic personality. And Mick credits the inimitable Ossie with the funniest, albeit one of the most serious and dangerous, off-field escapade of them all. One morning, Mick picked up a tabloid newspaper to see splashed all over it a lurid headline that read "England star in car crash – mystery blonde seen running from the scene."

Says Mick: "As sure as I was that the 10-1-on shot would win at one of the race meetings later that day, I was even more certain that the England star in this would be none other than my old mate Ossie."

And so it proved. Osgood and his then girlfriend, Pippa, were coming back from a night out and heading down the M3 in his beloved 2.5-litre purple Ford Capri, number plate 9 PO, when he came off at the junction at Bagshot in Berkshire and clipped the kerb. The car careered into a field and began to roll over and over. Fortunately, no other vehicles were involved in the accident but the car was smashed up and likely to ignite at any moment. So Ossie, who admitted that he had drunk well over the limit, started to sober up fast.

Young Michael at eight months. He was a contented baby (courtesy of Mrs Betty Channon).

Michael sits between older brother John and younger brother Phillip. The donkey belonged to Mr Grant, the friendly local farmer who allowed all the village children to have a ride. Michael's father keeps a watchful look-out (courtesy of Mrs Betty Channon).

The three Channon boys were all very active and enjoyed their sport, though they weren't so keen on their hair being cut by a local man in the village (courtesy of Mrs Betty Channon).

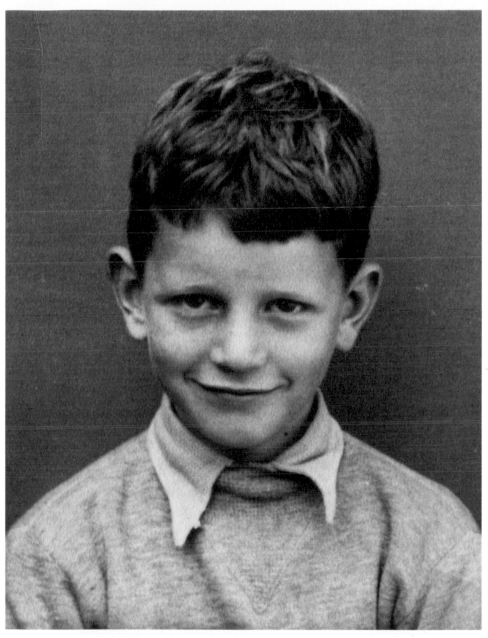

A school photograph of eight-year-old Michael (courtesy of Mrs Betty Channon).

Michael was very attached to the family pet, a pig affectionately named Spud. The boys would pull the pig up to their father's allotment on a purpose-built trolley (courtesy of Mrs Betty Channon).

Dreaming of the open road on his aunt's scooter (courtesy of Mrs Betty Channon).

*The Channon brothers pay Father Christmas a visit on a shopping
trip to Salisbury (courtesy of Mrs Betty Channon).*

*Flowers festoon the grave of Mick's older brother, John, who died suddenly in
an accident, aged just 14. Mick was ten years old at the time and he still
feels a very strong connection to his brother (courtesy of Mrs Betty Channon).*

Young Michael excelled at athletics, as the high jump photograph and pole vault certificate reveal (courtesy of Mrs Betty Channon).

Wiltshire Schools Athletic Association

Salisbury and South Wilts Area.

FIRST

Awarded to *M. Channon*

Event *Pole Vault 13-15*   *R H Iffman* Chairman

Date *May 30th, 1963*   *B Smeardon* Hon. Sec.

G.P. WILTON.

Mick (above, third from right) thoroughly enjoyed his time as a boy scout and adored the additional sporting opportunities (below) that presented themselves (courtesy of Mrs Betty Channon).

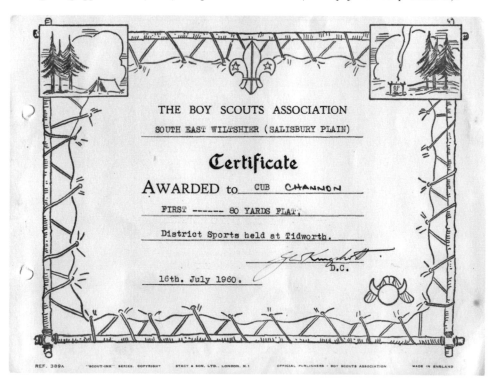

THE BOY SCOUTS ASSOCIATION

SOUTH EAST WILTSHIER (SALISBURY PLAIN)

Certificate

AWARDED to CUB CHANNON

FIRST ------ 80 YARDS FLAT,

District Sports held at Tidworth.

D.C.

16th. July 1960.

REF. 389A   "SCOUT-INK" SERIES. COPYRIGHT   STACY & SON. LTD., LONDON. N.1   OFFICIAL PUBLISHERS - BOY SCOUTS ASSOCIATION   MADE IN ENGLAND

A key part of the evidently successful Amesbury School football side (courtesy of Mrs Betty Channon)

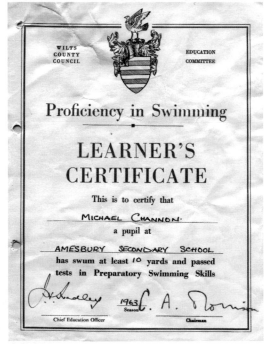

No doubt young Michael was relieved to have proof that he could swim 'at least 10 yards' (courtesy of Mrs Betty Channon).

"Act normal," he hissed at the shell-shocked young lady. "Get on the road and nip back to your house." According to Ossie, Pippa did just that whilst he leapt a hedge and ran off in the opposite direction towards the nearest pub. First thing the next morning, assuming that the alcohol would be out of his system, Ossie went to Chertsey police station and reported the accident. The desk sergeant appeared happy to see him and he soon found out why because although he had not been named, a photograph of the wrecked car was all over the papers with the personalised number plate clearly visible. So it did not take the head of MI5 to work out that 9 PO must have had something do with a famous centre-forward who lived thereabouts.

Later that morning Osgood took the train down to Southampton's ground and the first man waiting for him was his mate Mick, who could not stop giggling at the sight of Osgood.

"So, who's been a naughty boy then, Ossie?" laughs Mick.

"How's that, Mick?" says Ossie.

"Well it says in my paper that a mystery blonde and a footballer had been seen running away from the crash and that the blonde was 30 yards in front of the footballer and extending her lead with every stride so I knew the player couldn't possibly be anyone but you."

At that point the dressing room erupted. And when Mick posted the cutting on the changing-room wall he had pencilled a T in between the P and the O. His pal took the bait and said: "OK, what's the T for, Mick?"

"Please turn over," says Channon. " 'Cos there's more Ossie words and pictures about you on the next page," he lied.

The irrepressible Ossie and Lawrie McMenemy's other big-name signings were to transform eventually the Saints as-near-as-damn-it into as close to a glamour team as a small-town club could ever hope to get. Maybe it was the fact that Lawrie himself had only ever played in the lower leagues that made him such a stargazer or, more probably, he was an extremely shrewd man who had a vision of what he wanted to achieve and stuck to that ideal. It paid off so handsomely for him that at one time he held the record as English club football's longest-serving manager.

CHAPTER THIRTEEN
PUNTING PALS

It was not only Ale House Lads and chalk jockeys who befriended Channon in his days at Southampton. He also had his punting pals. The closest of these was a Southampton taxi driver known locally as Larry the Cab. Although in this case it was mainly Mick who did the befriending and not the other way around. It was his compassion and penchant for helping people unluckier in life than himself that must have drawn Mick to this big, affable fellow, whose real name was Bob Charles.

Like Mick himself, Charles had been something of a teenage sensation as the Southampton and England Youth goalkeeper. But he had smashed the bones in his left arm in three places in a collision during a match and was forced to retire from the game long before he reached his prime. After the belated success of Cathy Jane, Mick began forming small owners' syndicates with some of his Southampton and England team-mates and Bob was appointed as, to use his own words, "both manager and 'gofer' for these little firms." The first one with which they tried their luck was called Spill The Beans. All these years later, Mick cannot resist a rueful grin as he reminds himself: "That was the most aptly-named horse in the history of racing because my indiscreet fellow owners made sure every Southampton player, every England player and, it seemed, most of the Southampton and England fans knew when this one was expected to win.

"She only ever ran twice, though. She was placed both times but, sadly, she broke a leg and had to be put down. But owning her taught me the hard way that, like most other insiders in racing, I would have to make sure that I kept strictly 'schtum' about my horses' prospects in future. This was not strictly from the greed point of view, in that I didn't want the odds to shorten with half the country in the know, but also, hand on heart, to save me the cringing embarrassment of having to apologise to all and sundry if I said I fancied them and then they went and got beaten."

Then, as if anticipating that I would surely attempt to pick his brains soon, too, he adds: "And that rule still applies today. It stops me making enemies."

It was with this philosophy uppermost in mind that Mick pulled off what he still regards as the most successfully-managed coup of his short-lived, serious-gambling career. This came about after another hard lesson that resulted in a few burnt fingers. It began with another syndicate, when they paid £6,000 for a prospective jumper named Spark Off, with each member contributing £750, which was quite a hefty sum in the late 1970s. Spark Off was trained in Devon by another of Mick's close friends, John Baker. He had already won on the Flat when they bought him but they had him schooled over fences.

"He was fancied by the stable when we first ran him at Chepstow in a televised race and naturally the syndicate members were very excited," says Mick. "They had their fivers and tenners each way; and some, a good deal more. We took the precaution of booking top jockey Jonjo O'Neill to ride. But the horse just did not jump a hurdle properly and nearly pulled up at one of them. I have never felt so embarrassed in my life. It was worse than playing like a dipstick yourself in a football match.

"He had run too badly to be true and finished tailed-off. Back at John Baker's yard, they could not understand it either. And this turned out to be an early punting lesson for me in that, just like footballers, horses are not machines and have their on and off days. "Taking a lesson from his own profession, Mick reckoned that practice would make perfect and asked John to school Spark Off more intensely. He was taken to Taunton racecourse and schooled over the bigger fences with another horse and improved immeasurably. So much so that Mick was convinced that he only had to skip over the hurdles and he was a racing certainty in the right company. "But," says Mick, "this time I decided to keep my opinion to myself. I would not have been able to face another embarrassment like that first flop. All I had to work on was my own private conviction after seeing that workout with my own eyes and I felt that was enough. So I told Bob Charles that we were going to fill our boots on him next time out."

Bob Charles takes up the story here: "When I asked Mick what size boots we were going to have on, he replied: 'We are going to have our bollocks on.' "And this meant Mick going so far as to borrow money off his dad and brother.

Spark Off was entered at Devon and Exeter on New Year's Day 1980. Southampton happened to be playing Arsenal that day at 11 o'clock in the morning and Lawrie McMenemy had taken Mick and the other lads to the Southampton Post House Hotel for the night – New Year's Eve or no New Year's Eve. Mick had asked me to get his money on all over town in bits and pieces. Obviously, that was because we wanted the biggest price we could get and we didn't want the news of a big bet getting back to the course. At a little track like Devon and Exeter even a couple of hundred pounds could turn a 20 to 1 chance into favourite in no time. And Mick didn't want just a 'bottle' (£200) on, he wanted to win the price of a nice house or, more precisely, a little stud farm.

"I shot round to the Post House to get the money off Mick on New Year's Eve, resisted the temptation to blow it all on an almighty piss-up – only joking – and made myself busy next morning. And I mean busy: I must have put bets on in more than 30 betting shops in and around Southampton and my old taxi had never stopped and started more often than that before or has since. To make it even more difficult, Devon and Exeter was the only meeting not to be called off that day due to the freezing weather. This meant that more attention than normal was being paid by the betting shop clerks to this one meeting and, to avoid suspicion from the people there who knew I was a pal of Mick's, I had to keep making up little cock and bull stories that I was only putting the bets on for my mother-in-law, my grandma and Old Uncle Tom Cobley and all. Ironically, Mick told me later that the pitch for his match had been rock hard and that he couldn't believe our race could possibly be given the go-ahead.

"It was, though, and Spark Off stormed home at a starting price of 12 to 1. Mick won more than £7,000, which was big dough then, but all he could keep saying afterwards was how guilty he felt because he hadn't told the other lads that he fancied the horse. That was typical of him. Mick Channon is the most generous man I've ever met in my life. I love him and so does my wife. When she was ill with cancer, Mick sent her flowers every single day – that's the sort of caring, sharing bloke he is."

One other little betting story that remains lodged in Mick's memory in a perverse way concerns the time he and Peter Osgood backed Mick's horse Jamesmead in the Cesarewitch – a lucky race for him, or so he thought, because it produced his very first winning punt when he was still a teenager. He explains: "We were playing at The Dell that same day and the race was due off about half an hour after our kick-off time. So we had arranged for one of Ossie's mates to signal the result from the stands. And, sure enough, as I went to take a throw-in, there was this big, red-haired bloke jumping up and down in his seat and sticking two fingers up at me. I must admit I was shocked, I thought: 'OK, maybe I'm not on tip-top form today but I can't be playing that fucking badly, surely!' It was only when Ossie nudged me later on and said: 'We finished second, then,' that I remembered what the guy had obviously meant with that dodgy hand signal."

CHAPTER FOURTEEN

ENGLAND

When Mick Channon's old punting pal, Kevin Keegan, found the job of being England manager too much for him and resigned suddenly a few years back, one of the main criticisms levelled at him was the amount of off-duty card playing in which he allowed his players to indulge. But Mick contends that as an ex-England star himself Keegan was simply doing what came naturally. Channon was an England regular for more than five years under four different managers and found that playing cards for money came as naturally as breathing to almost every member of every squad he was ever in.

On the very first day he reported for training with England, he says he was pulled aside by Frannie Lee and invited to join him, Geoff Hurst and Martin Peters in a seven-card brag school. The stakes were a fiver a time and this made him so nervous that, in his own words: "I almost shit myself." Even though he was already a gambling man, that kind of stake was way out of Southampton's league.

"I had to join in because I didn't want to be labelled a wimp," he adds. "The tradition seemed to be that the bigger you got in the football game, the bigger the big-time Charlie you had to become." It would certainly seem that betting and boozing was so endemic in the British working-class way of life that there was no way a British manager was ever going to even think about changing things. Mick says now: "I hear that Sven is trying to put a stop to the punting but I have to warn him that when Don Revie tried it in my day he came unstuck. He wanted to keep the stakes down, so he introduced drawn-out games like putting, carpet bowls and bingo. But even though I couldn't play golf to save my life, I still skinned him for £250 one day on the putting. He was the bookie and he quoted me at 25 to 1. But he had underestimated my competitive gambling instincts and I won the tournament after having had a tenner on myself."

Of all the gambling men who ever pulled on an England shirt, Stan Bowles must have been the most notorious. But Mick remembers one of Stan's more harmless gambling anecdotes with feelings of empathy. It was shortly after Revie had introduced his infamous pre-match dossiers. They were lengthy documents that included an admiring analysis on every member of the opposing team. And each England man was required to memorise every detail then act upon it during the upcoming game. "They were so flattering to the opposition that they tended to frighten the life out of you," says Mick. "So the likes of Stan and myself simply threw them into the waste-paper baskets in our room. For my part, I was too busy reading my breeding brochures, anyway."

It so happened that before an important World Cup qualifying match against Italy in Rome in 1976 Bowles was sharing a room with the young right-back, Dave Clement, who was tragically to commit suicide when his career was over. "Dear old Dave was keen as mustard and kept reading and re-reading the dreaded dossier in his room then reciting it aloud and asking Stan questions about it," recalls Mick.

"The night before the game some of us were playing cards in the hotel to take our minds off tomorrow. And like the good little lads we were pretending to be under Don, we agreed that the last hand should be dealt at 11 o'clock and no later – no matter how much anyone was losing. Well, when one of the lads called: 'Time gentlemen, please', Stan got down on his knees and begged us to carry on playing. It turned out that it wasn't that Stan was determined to recoup his losses, it was just that he was afraid Dave would keep him awake all night reading out that dodgy fucking dossier!"

England went on to lose that particular match 2-0 and Revie's world fell apart. Shortly afterwards he jumped ship, just as Keegan was to do more than 20 years later and he forsook the England team during a tour of South America, going off to hold talks in Saudi Arabia in order to secure his financial future by managing in Dubai.

I first got to know Mick Channon, Kevin Keegan and their generation of England players when we toured together for Sir Alf Ramsey's England Under-23 team. We were closeted in the same hotels, planes and bars for ten days to a fortnight. Unlike their seniors, with whom most of us pressmen had already shared adventures all over the world together, readers were not biting their fingernails over the results of these young England matches. But our sports editors knew these trips were invaluable for making contact with these up-and-coming stars that would turn out to be more than useful for our papers in years to come. Indeed, it was on these tours that I first struck up friendships with some of them that were to last a lifetime. In the cases of Mick, Kevin, Alan Ball, Peter Osgood, Frannie Lee and Peter Shilton, these friendships extended to finding myself in their company on numerous off-duty days at the races together.

And as if to prove the point, during one of my subsequent periods of unemployment, Kevin tipped me off exclusively about his transfer from Liverpool to Hamburg because he knew I was in dire need of the freelance earnings the story would bring me. One such tour took us to Kiev in the old Soviet Union, where we were badly bitten by relatives of the same bed bugs who once took lumps out of Princess Anne when she represented the British Equestrian team there. On this occasion, as we piled off the team bus at the hotel, we all found ourselves in need of after-match drinks of varying description. And, in dear old Alf's case, it was a quintessential English cup of tea.

I shall never forget how Sir Alf's elocution lessons went out of the window as he attempted to get it. His efforts to communicate with the aged night porter, in his shabby old uniform, got nowhere. But, true to character, Alf was determined to have his way and commissar after commissar was summoned to join in the conversation. Eventually, Alf got his tea, but with a lemon and no milk. He got no joy with that word either and, exasperated, he was reduced to attempting a feeble but angry charade in which he gave an impression of a milkmaid at work whilst shouting: "Cow! Cow! Tits! Tits! Fucking great tits!"

In Mick's case it was a vodka session with the rest of the lads. And, in true country-boy style, he entertained them with a rendering or two of a yokel song that began with the line: "I rise at six to feed the chicks". He was followed by hippy Frank Worthington, whose way-out mode of dress horrified Alf when he first clapped eyes on it. Frank did his customary 'Blue Suede Shoes' Elvis impression. Unfortunately, the party by this time had spilled out on to a balcony and one or two full glasses were knocked off it, drenching some Ukranian citizens below.

This meant that Alf had to be roused from his bed to restore order and Mick says that the rowdiest boys were all terrified that they would not get picked again. "But I needn't have worried," says Mick. "Alf sensed that there was nothing malicious in our antics and that we were just a bunch of high-spirited young lads unwinding. So I survived that scare and went on to win nine Under-23 caps before getting into the senior squad."

And he adds: "This was the equivalent of breaking into the Bank of England in those days. That's how stingy Alf was with dishing out full England caps. He certainly didn't toss them around like confetti as is the case these days. And as for the captain's armband – on the couple of occasions I wore it, they would have had to administer anaesthetic and perform an operation to prise it off me. Once you got into Alf's squad you knew you were going to get a fair crack at it. And that if you were good enough you would have the chance of a decent run in the team. That took a long time, though. But as a wise, old farmhand once said to me: 'When God invented time, he invented a lot of it' and that old saying stood me in good stead then and later in the racing game, where you have to be patient, particularly with two-year-olds.

"You had to spend a year of night matches in the stand – not even as a substitute in the final 16. Alf took a bloody long look at you both in training and at the way you conducted yourself with your team-mates off the field. The result of all this was that by the time your chance came, you weren't shy any more, the complexes were conquered and you weren't afraid to join in the traditional mickey-taking. It all added up to being thoroughly bedded in."

True to form, Mick had to wait a year before winning his first full cap. It came almost 18 months after England's unlucky exit from the 1970 World Cup in Mexico, which I was privileged to cover. Mick's debut was against Yugoslavia at Wembley in October

1972. The match ended in a 1-1 draw with Mick's Manchester City team-mate-to-be, Joe Royle, scoring the goal. Four months later Channon became a regular after England beat Scotland 5-0 in their centenary match on their own ice-covered Hampden Park pitch during which he scored the first of his 21 goals for England to add to the three he had notched for the Under-23s and the two more he netted for Football League representative elevens.

After that Hampden triumph, he then played in the next four England matches – only to be left out of the June 1973 World Cup qualifying game in Poland, which England lost 2-0. Sir Alf decided to play with an extra midfield man – Arsenal's tough-tackling Peter Storey – and leave out one of the strikers, namely Mick. He was recalled for the next match, a 2-1 win over the Soviet Union in Moscow, where he gave what he regards as his best-ever England performance and after which Alf admitted that he had made a mistake in not playing Channon in Poland.

It is now a matter of history how unlucky England were not to beat the Poles in that vital last qualifying match for the 1974 World Cup, at Wembley in 1973, and how well the Poles went on to play in the finals. Still suffering from regret all these years later, Mick says:"It was such a shame we missed out. Those triumphant 1966 lads, Bobby Moore, Alan Ball and Martin Peters, were still going strong. My old Southampton team-mate, Martin Chivers, was in sharp form up front with me and Allan Clarke of Leeds. We had two great goalkeepers in Peter Shilton and Ray Clemence and Roy McFarland of Derby was a magnificent centre-half. Since then, though, I've learned to take the hard knocks on the chin, especially in racing, which, as everyone involved in the sport knows, is a game that tames lions."

After Sir Alf was sacked, Mick went on to play regularly for England during Joe Mercer's tenure as caretaker manager and then, of course, throughout Don Revie's reign. As for Revie's successor, Ron Greenwood, Mick says philosophically: "He just didn't seem to fancy me – so that was that."

He is loath to let go of his England memoirs, however, without recalling one horrific incident that happened to Kevin Keegan under Joe Mercer. Setting the scene, he says: "We were on a tour to East Germany, Bulgaria and Yugoslavia during the summer of 1974 with dear old jovial Joe in charge when, on arrival at Belgrade Airport, Kevin got really badly beaten up by the local police and then arrested. It didn't quite make the kind of sensational headlines as the infamous Bobby Moore and the bracelet incident in Bogota a few years earlier, but it almost caused an international incident.

"Kevin had bought a fragile gift to take home and as the luggage came round on the conveyor belt, he stepped over one package to get to his own. With that, all hell broke loose. A member of the secret police dragged him off and started roughing him up. Kevin tried to motion to the guy not to be so bloody silly but three other plain-clothes cops grabbed him too. I joined in the general protest but the heavies manhandled him out of the baggage area and there was nothing we could do about stopping them. We found out later that he had been punched and generally done over in a brutal way.

"We held a players' meeting on the spot, threatening to go home there and then. But even Joe and the FA officials were unable to reason with the authorities there. It was a police state then and that seemed to be that, as far as they were concerned – tough shit!

"Those were the days, eh?"

CHAPTER FIFTEEN

WORLD'S END

During my 40 years of professional involvement with sport there have been, in my opinion, three truly black-armband days for English football. They were the 1953 tutorial from Hungary, when the immortal magical Magyars, as they were popularly known, inflicted on England a first-ever defeat on home soil by the world-shattering scoreline of 6-3.

Then there was the 3-2, extra-time, quarter-final defeat by the old enemy West Germany in the scorching heat of Leon, Mexico, during the 1970 World Cup after Ramsey's heroes had appeared to be shooing in after going two goals up. And last but certainly not the least painful was the autumnal night in October 1973 when the 100,000 people packed into the old Wembley Stadium could only stare in disbelief as England trooped off the field after a 1-1 draw with Poland that plunged England into the World Cup wilderness for the rest of the 1970s and virtually ended the careers of England's greatest-ever manager, Sir Alf Ramsey, and greatest-ever captain, Bobby Moore.

On the very rare occasions on which football made the front pages of our newspapers back in the 1970s it was usually when George Best was either pulling a Miss World or pissing on his unique talent. But on the fateful morning of 18 October, my own paper *The Sun* led its late editions with huge headlines proclaiming "The End Of The World". And that was exactly how it felt to Mick Channon and the rest of his England team-mates who had, on the previous evening, taken part in what was arguably the most one-sided drawn game in the history of association football.

It was the never-to-be-forgotten night when they came up against a gangling, awkward-looking giant of a man named Jan Tomaszewski whose hands, feet, knees, elbows and backside, and with more than a little bit of help from his crossbar and uprights, kept out no fewer than 31 genuinely goal-bound efforts from the English – nine of which came from Channon alone. "Tomasz" the Terrible was otherwise known as "Cloughie's Clown" after old big 'ead himself had given him that unenviable epithet in an assessment as a television panellist.

And Brian's bloomer was not the only English mistake of that night of mishaps. Poland's goal came via a once-in-a-lifetime balls-up of a tackle from Norman "bites yer legs" Hunter and an equally rare error from goalkeeper Peter Shilton, who dived over the top of the Polish goalscorer's daisy-cutting shot. And so strong was the sense of irony that pervaded that old Wembley fortress on this nightmare of a night that from first minute to last every soul in the stadium, with the exception of Comrade "Tomasz", expected England to find the Polish net at any given second of the one-sided action. That they had to content themselves with a solitary penalty conversion from Allan "Sniffer" Clarke of Leeds United seemed beyond human comprehension. History was to present us with one minute crumb of consolation, however, when in the finals of that tournament, which was staged in West Germany the following summer, Poland turned out to be unrecognisable from the mugs Cloughie and his cohorts had suspected them to be by finishing third behind the Germans and the Dutch.

For English football fans everywhere, that Polish debacle was to live in the memory as one of those "where-were-you-when?" occasions. And Mrs Jane Channon recalls it as the one and only time her husband ever brought his work home to such a shattering extent. "Mick was much more than depressed," she recalls. "If we had kept a cat, I'm sure he would have kicked it all over the house."

As it was, that result meant that when the World Cup finals stage came around, he could only kick his his heels in frustration. And that is a particularly sore point for the man himself, whose main memory of that miserable match was having a first-half goal, which was deflected into the Polish net off his heel, mysteriously disallowed. Incidentally, if that goal had stood, it would have ranked as a museum piece alongside the goal he made for England when they beat world champions West Germany 2–0 in a Wembley friendly 17 months later. On this occasion, he set up one of the English goals by sneaking a free-kick to Alan Ball whilst his body was still on the turf after the offending German tackle. His pal Bally duly crossed to the far post where Malcolm "Supermac" Macdonald leapt to head it past the surprised German goalkeeper.

Before his England career eventually came to a close, Channon was to score 21 times for his country, a record that puts him in joint-twelfth place on the all-time list of England goalscorers alongside his other old buddy Kevin Keegan. And Kevin will wince when I remind him here that Mick's total came in 46 matches whereas Kevin had to make 63 appearances to equal it.

Channon's England career really flourished under Don Revie, who made no secret of his admiration for the Saints idol by saying time and time again that Mick was every manager's dream forward because he could and did strike from anywhere across the front line and was equally happy going through the middle or haring down the wing. And Revie twice went as far as making Mick captain from that position, which was a revolutionary move in those days of conventional stopper-centre-half skippers. Interesting that, when you remember that Revie made his own playing name in his revolutionary deep-lying, centre-forward role for Manchester City a la Hidegkuti of Hungary.

And this is the area in which Mick himself can finally pin down for us the exact birth of that mysterious windmill celebration. He started it, he says, back in his early days at Southampton when Ted Bates used him as a lone striker in the bizarre 1–9–1 formation Bates used to favour in those days. Mick says now: "The fact that I was up front on my own meant that most of my goals followed long runs from me which left me breathless and knackered and I used to swing my arm to get some air back into my lungs, to relieve the tension and, let's be honest here, to be a bit flash like I was when I was cheering on my winners at the races." So there it is: the definitive explanation of Mick's windmill-arm celebration, straight from the horse's mouth, as it were.

It was an even bigger compliment to Channon that Revie made him an automatic choice, when it was the very uncertainty of his selection system that ruined his own England managerial career. He was forever chopping and changing his men and bowing to media pressure by choosing whichever potential new boy was the press's flavour of the month when the team was picked. And, of course, he earned unrivalled notoriety by demonstrating just how final his indecision was when he once selected more than 50 players for an England get-together. Shades of Sven-Goran Eriksson here, I hear you cry. Yes, but there did seem to be a lot more method in the Swedish ice man's apparent madness than in dear old Don's.

And as far as Mick is concerned, he is still trying to fathom Revie's reasoning for that irrational round-up of England's finest. "Mind you, I was not complaining because all us lads had the mother and father of a piss-up meeting old friends and enemies like that. It was even better than the annual gathering of the clans at the Football Writers' Player of the Year dinner. Can you imagine what it was like when the Don told us he wanted to get us all off to bed early on that Saturday night? We'd all been involved in League games that afternoon and to forsake the traditional letting-the-hair-down ritual that every man jack of us always indulged in, was nothing short of sacrilege on his part. His point was that he wanted to get us all back to our clubs bright-eyed and bushy-tailed so he thought that this Horlicks and cocoa early-night nonsense was in order – some chance!

"I'm not saying that absolutely everyone got paralytic that night but it was any price you like about finding any of us sober. The other guests in the hotel were in danger of being trampled to death in the rush as the boys gave Don a collective up-yours message and scampered out to play night games in the pubs and clubs of Manchester. Miraculously, we all managed to muster in time for Revie's ridiculous get-together on the Sunday before making our way very gingerly back to our various home clubs.

"Incidentally, Revie did not particularly endear himself to us much at that meeting either, when he gave what he must have imagined was his version of Shakespeare's Henry the Fifth speech by stressing that he demanded that we call him boss whenever we addressed him and that we were punctual whenever he summoned us to his presence."

Ron Greenwood brought a cerebral, professorial air to his reign as Revie's successor and he did not appear to favour Channon's rough-and-ready personality nor his hell-for-leather greyhound-like playing style. Or maybe he just didn't fancy Mick's long legs. For as a gangly, six feet-tall, pathetic parks player myself, who was miles slower than Teddy Sheringham and turned about as swiftly as a fully-laden articulated lorry, I distinctly remember thinking that there was hope for me yet when Ron told me one day that he had shortened peerless Martin Peters' youthful, long, loping stride by making him run backwards in training every day for years. On a personal level, Greenwood was to snub Channon whenever their paths crossed occasionally in the years to come, after Mick had criticised his management style on television.

And it was during his stint as a TV panellist that Mick made more enemies than in the rest of his life put together. "I was publicly very critical of England's management during those World Cup famine years and once you started criticising people the television viewers did seem to expect it from you on a regular basis. So, on reflection, perhaps I did go over the top a bit too much. But I still stand by every word of what I said about Greenwood and that sickening World Cup failure in Spain when two of our best players, Kevin and Trevor Brooking, were left out of the starting line-up even though they had declared themselves fit after recent injuries. In the event they were not brought off the substitutes' bench until far too late to save our World Cup necks.

"I have played in more than 900 first-class games but if I had waited until I was fully fit each time, I wouldn't have reached 200. The best players forget niggling injury problems and play through them. And as a manager you are entitled to take their word for the level of fitness they are at and hold your hands up and put them out on the park where they belong."

You may, like me, wonder why Mick took his television work so seriously when he is the first to admit that he thinks that what clinched that job for him was his country yokel's accent, of which most viewers delighted in making fun. Although nobody laughs when Mick is asked to discuss his horses on the box these days. He says: "Personally, I never worry for a moment if I am criticised. If I cared about that sort of thing I'd never get out of bed in the morning." That, incidentally, is a feat in itself when you consider how much damage his football career did to his legs and feet.

But in the 1985-86 season he talked his way into a serious dispute when the then England and Manchester United goalkeeper, Gary Bailey, complained to the Professional Footballers' Association about Channon's criticism of both his game and his attitude towards it. Mick explains: "I thought Gary had a soft side to him that made him want to be liked all the time. Now, to my mind, you can't go through life always being liked by everyone; nobody can. It's dog-eat-dog in the competitive world of football." In response to Bailey's complaint, Mick received a letter from Players' Union secretary Gordon Taylor. Mick remembers that piece of correspondence well. "It was saying that he was sure the press had exaggerated certain remarks I had made about Gary," says Mick, "and that he felt sure I hadn't said all those things. But the next time I saw Taylor I told him straight that I had meant every word I said about Bailey and that I would go on permanent record by admitting it."

One of life's certainties, well beyond dispute, is that Mick Channon definitely does not call a spade a shovel.

CHAPTER SIXTEEN

MANCHESTER CITY

It was beside a hotel swimming pool on the edge of Copacabana Beach where a lazy day in the sun became the turning point for a dramatic change in Mick Channon's life. On the morning after starring for England in a goalless draw against Brazil at the legendary Maracana Stadium in June 1977 he was sunning himself with the other England players when he was – not to put too fine a point on it – well and truly nobbled. Not that he minded, because the man doing the nobbling was about to offer him a deal that was to make him the highest-paid player in England at that time.

The late Peter Swales was the all-powerful chairman of Manchester City and a leading member of the official FA party on that tour and the team was managed by the late Don Revie. Mick's pal, Kevin Keegan, remembers the incident this way: "It was the most blatant tap-up job I've ever seen. Peter approached Mick in front of everyone. It was so obvious, that we began chiding Mick: 'Off to Manchester City, then, are we mate?'

And he was – he signed for them the next month."

Swales would, of course, have been "hung, drawn and quartered" for that if he had been reported to the authorities, but the times they were a-changing by then, anyway. Revie was setting up the shady deal that was to see him scarper off to the anonymity of the desert in Dubai and Keegan had just been transferred to Hamburg in one of the very first big transfer deals to be conducted through an agent. That same agent, incidentally, offered Channon a £60,000 signing-on-fee plus around £50,000 a year basic to join Bordeaux. But at 28 and in his prime, country-boy Mick was nowhere near ready to go abroad for his living and even less inclined to pay the agent ten per cent of all monies involved. Instead, he found himself in Swales' lovely house in Altrincham, Cheshire, nervously listening to an offer that had him tingling with excited anticipation. He was being lured by a three-year contract at £43,000 a year and £100 a point and playing for a team like City, who had finished runners-up in the top division in the previous season, that meant an almost guaranteed 60 points a season.

So at £1000 a week he became the highest-paid player in this country. Not a lot, compared to David Beckham's £100,000 a week now, but big enough bucks three decades ago. And with the money City were also paying into a pension fund for him it meant that he would never have to draw the dole no matter what might befall him in later life. But the record £300,000 transfer fee City paid for Channon was broken only a few days later when Liverpool signed Kenny Dalglish from Celtic.

Today, Mick still has the greatest respect for Swales. "I couldn't help admiring his quest to be the best and his lifelong desire to put one over on his neighbours at Old Trafford," he says, "If that was wrong then there are an awful lot of people who've got a different opinion to me on the subject. I know he had his critics, that people said he was a dictator and that his kind of wheeling and dealing proved to be suicidal for City in the end. But I still give him full marks for trying." What poetic irony, then, that when Mick's old England colleague Frannie Lee made the final phone call that brought him control of City from Swales, these two old playmates just happened to be sharing a bottle of champagne together on holiday at Frannie's house in Barbados.

Mick maintains: "City were a great club when I was there. Nothing was too much trouble for anyone as far as looking after the players was concerned. The whole staff, from the secretary down to the groundsman and the tea lady, were tremendous. The only problem I had, at first, was on the pitch. To put it bluntly, I wasn't worth two bob." To make matters worse there was a struggle between the players for the top-dog spot – was it to be Dennis Tueart, Joe Royle, my own special little mate Asa Hartford, Peter Barnes or Mick Channon? And, according to Mick, City became a bunch of talented individuals rather than a team, because the manager, Tony Book, was not a very strong character. And that power struggle amongst the players spilled out on to the pitch, where everyone started pulling in different directions.

Mick still explodes at the memory. "I only seemed to get a touch of the ball when everybody else was finished with it. And because I was quick and needed the ball early, it was no good to anybody. Forwards need time to create something so the earlier I got the ball, the better. Say, for instance, that in one second I could run ten yards – and I was quicker than Linford Christie over that first ten – in half a second five yards and so on; in a sixteenth of a second, I could run half a yard.

"What do you need to score goals? The answer is a split second. That means if you can get the ball a second earlier, you've probably got five to ten yards to work in. So one hundredth of a second is probably the equivalent of an inch, which may be a case of getting your toe there and scoring before a defender can get a tackle in. That is how important time can be and it didn't suit me the way we were playing. It wasn't the flowing type of game that I was used to – I just couldn't adjust that quickly. Dennis wanted the game played to suit him because he was a wide player, Peter Barnes likewise, and he also wanted to take the lace out of the ball. I wasn't getting a kick and when I did, I was having to turn myself inside out."

To cap everything, not long after he arrived at City, Channon sustained the worst setback of his career – a pelvic strain that kept him out of action for six weeks. On reflection, he reckons he was lucky because he recovered from that particular problem and it was one that had finished a lot of players' careers. For a while, and for the first time in his life, football became a nightmare for him. When he returned to the first team, he remembers being kicked black and blue on the field and enduring terrible verbal abuse off it. He remembers: "There were chants from the terraces of 'What a waste of money' and I had only been there six months. I determined that I would either have to curl up and die or dig in and fight my way through it. I dug in to the extent that I'm certain that my time at Maine Road made me grow up as a person. Football-wise, I didn't have a very good time but I had to fight the world and it turned me from a rather spoilt boy into a man."

Such were the pressures at City that Mick had to be so fully committed to his soccer career that his favourite hobby of "ducking and diving" at the racetracks had to be abandoned. But he managed to maintain his breeding interests by retaining his little stud at Lower Chase Farm, not far from his country roots in Swanmore, where brother Phil looked after the four broodmares that still included Cathy Jane.

Strangely enough, it was when Malcolm Allison arrived at

City to begin his second spell as manager there that Mick's form and fortunes took a distinct turn for the better. Although he never rated the man as a manager and was destined to fall out with the larger-than-life "Big Mal" in a big way, he responded to the challenge of this new managerial broom by sweeping in 11 goals in Allison's first 13 games in charge. He still says: "It was easier to understand the film *One Flew Over the Cuckoo's Nest* than to make head or tail of Malcolm's tactics. For me, the simple reason that the big man made his name as coach at City the first time around was because he had great players in the likes of Frannie Lee, Mike Summerbee and Colin Bell. The second time around he made the mistake of thinking that it was him and his tactics that made a team and not the players.

"He was always wanting to put square pegs in round holes and I thought he had finally disappeared up his own arse when, on the next pre-season tour, he came up with another new playing toy to satisfy his strange curiosity. The toy concerned was a lad called Barry Silkman, who has since made a name for himself as a greyhound trainer and a soccer agent, but who, on his arrival at City, had come as a virtually unknown winger via Hereford, Crystal Palace and Plymouth. Big Mal's brainwave was to play Barry as a continental-style sweeper and I soon let him know that this was the most ridiculous experiment I had ever experienced in my life whereupon he blew his top and promptly hoicked me around as being available for transfer."

On the face of it, as Channon and Allison were so often seen joking together on the television, it must have appeared to the sporting public that the pair were indeed two of a kind – extroverts singing from the same soccer hymn sheet. That is how their working relationship began but by the end of it they could barely stand the sight of each other. They may not have been aware of it but to an onlooker, like myself, it was obvious that this was a clash between two control freaks. The only difference between them was that Channon only wanted to control himself and his own destiny whereas Allison wanted to control the world and everyone in it. And if Channon's ego was a little on the large side at that time, Allison's self-regard was positively gargantuan.

Inevitably, it was to be Old Father Time who was to be the definitive judge of their personality clash. And for better or for worse, he found in favour of Channon – by a distance. For whilst Mick's star is still rising, Mal's has waned and wound down in the saddest way imaginable. After tipping the brim of that famous Fedora of his and puffing on a few more of those Havana cigars in various different managerial offices and boardrooms, I hear that he is now in poor health and living in impoverished circumstances. Now that is tragic. For although Mal may have been more full of himself than almost anybody I ever knew, he always had that charismatic quality of enhancing the lives he came into contact with, even if they did not appreciate it at the time.

For, in my view, being full of yourself is a very different thing from being selfish. And as well as being a taker, Big Mal was a giver – a giver of himself and he had plenty to give. He was never less than the very best of company whenever I was privileged to be with him. He also, ironically, loved a bet as much as Mick did.

CHAPTER SEVENTEEN
THE SECOND COMING

If you will forgive the minor blasphemy, among my favourite football stories is the one that claimed that when the slogan "What Will You Do When Jesus Comes to Liverpool?" was posted outside a church near Anfield, some wag had scrawled underneath it: "Move St John to centre-forward." Well, some of the more fanatical Saints fans of the 1970s had already invested Mick Channon with divine power by sporting a banner at every home game which read "Jesus saves – Channon nets the rebound." And his second coming to Southampton also had its biblical undertones. For, after being away from his spiritual home for two years, fans at The Dell gave him as warm a welcome as the prodigal son. Saints got him back for £175,000 – good value when set against the sum for which they had sold him to Manchester City. In this, his second spell as a Dell Boy, Mick found a very different Lawrie McMenemy from the one to whom he had waved goodbye.

Big Lawrie had grown into the job so quickly and come so far since his own departure that Mick began calling him "The Ayatollah". The first inkling Mick had that the Saints were interested in having him back came when Allison told him that as Southampton were playing at Old Trafford on the coming Saturday, McMenemy would like to see him whilst he was in Manchester. Mick takes up the story:"I certainly was a bit surprised because we had had our disagreements in the past. But sometimes you don't appreciate people or places until they're not there for you anymore. And I like to think that applied to Lawrie as much as me."

No sooner had he arrived back, than Alan Ball was signing for Saints after a successful stint for Vancouver Whitecaps in the North American Soccer League. "So," says Mick, "as one-time great pals in the England squad we teamed up again for three smashing years with the Saints during which we qualified for Europe twice. Then, to cap it all, the season after I returned, Lawrie snapped up my old England room-mate Kevin Keegan as well. It wasn't long before the three of us were back in harness as horse-racing partners."

Keegan's arrival at Southampton was the signal for one of the biggest media jamborees every staged over the signing-on of a player. Twice European Footballer of the Year by then, Kevin's departure from Hamburg had been so hush-hush that when McMenemy paraded such a superstar before the sports journalists and television cameras and told them that Keegan was joining homespun Southampton, the scene resembled the sight of a magician pulling a rabbit out of a top hat. Typically, though, it was a race meeting that took precedence over this big event as far as Mick was concerned. For by now Mick was up and running as an owner again and he had a horse entered at Wolverhampton on the day of the big signing. McMenemy had rung Mick, who was still living in Manchester and enjoying a day off at the time, to let him into the secret. But Mick replied:"I can see Kevin every day from now on, but I can't see my horse run." And he still insists he got his priorities right over that decision.

In the week before he left City for Southampton, Channon had received what he describes as "a very interesting offer" from the then Third Division Blackpool to become their player-manager. The legend of ex-Blackpool winger Sir Stanley Matthews was still magical enough to draw anyone to that famous old club, if only to take a peek at the contemporary set-up. Waiting for Mick in the boardroom was an elderly gentleman sporting a jet black toupee, which was the most obvious wig Mick had ever seen. But on the way to the job interview Mick had already decided that at 29 he was still too young to give up playing full-time. So he told the board of directors: "Gentlemen, before we go any further, it is very kind of you to invite me here for this interview, but I now feel that it's in the best interests of Blackpool and Mick Channon if I don't take the job. I feel I can carry on playing full-time for a few more years yet and it's important that you carry on with your task of finding a manager while I continue playing."

Suddenly, the chairman jumped up and exclaimed: "Oh, young man, I've been involved as a director in football for nearly 30 years and that is the most impressive speech I've ever heard from anyone. We'd love you to come and watch us play Bury tonight while we try and talk you round." Mick told the Blackpool board that it was a very kind invitation and that, by all means, he would go and watch them. So he did and both parties shook hands and left on very good terms. That was one of only two soccer managerial jobs in which Channon was ever interested ... the other interview came much later and was conducted by that arch-villain, the late Sir Robert Maxwell, at Oxford United.

In Kevin Keegan's first season at Saints, the club managed to scrape into Europe; although it was a close thing. The next season they started so well, though, that Mick talked the rest of the team into having a punt on their chances. In April – towards the end of the season – they were still several points clear at the top of the First Division but had played several more games than their nearest challengers. At a players' meeting, Mick persuaded his team-mates to stake £1,000 between them to win the championship at what he regarded were still "silly odds" of 16 to 1.

The only person who was not at the meeting was defender Chris Nicholl, who later went on to become the club manager. Mick relates: "I didn't think Chris would have a bet, but I voted him in anyway. It soon went pear-shaped, though, when we drew at Notts County and lost at Coventry. My name was mud in the dressing room for the rest of the season. But I knew then and I know now that unless you believe in your cause you won't win anything and too many of our lads lacked the self-belief to become champions. But, sadly, as we were real crowd pullers back then and played to packed houses every week, I'm sure that a lot of our fans must have done their money on us, too.

"They turned out to be three blinding years for me back at Southampton. The attraction wasn't just Kevin, although he was a great draw, but the attacking football we played was turning people on all over the country. In every game there seemed to be three or four goals at least. I scored the ITV goal of the season back then. The build-up to the goal was great, not just my finishing, and it came against all-conquering Liverpool, which made it that bit more special for us.

"We were such a nicely balanced side, too, with David Armstrong joining us from Middlesbrough and then making the England team, and young, bright-as-a-button Steve Williams coming through before joining Arsenal. But it all began to fall apart for us when Lawrie and Kevin fell out so badly that they never spoke to each other again for some years. Kevin had a very strong personality – strong enough to match Lawrie's – so I could sense things coming to a head between the pair of them. It was almost a replica of the situation between Terry Paine and Lawrie during my first spell at Southampton. The big difference this time, however, was that Kevin was by no means on the way out like Terry had been.

"As both Lawrie and Kevin were used to getting their own way, the big bust-up between them was inevitable. It came when we played Wolves in a Bank Holiday game towards the end of the season and got a rare home beating. We knew we had played badly and Lawrie stormed into the dressing room afterwards and told us we were useless and then added: 'You lot didn't even try today.' One of the lads muttered something by way of a reply and so did Kevin. And then Lawrie said: 'And that includes all of you.' Suddenly, Kevin snapped: 'What do you mean, I didn't try? That's something I've always done, right through my career.' Obviously, Kevin's pride had been hurt, but I still think he was wrong to react the way he did.

"Lawrie had said something in the heat of the moment, the sort of thing that happens thousands of times in dressing rooms after matches. The manager is entitled to have his say afterwards, especially when you've just taken a good beating at home. But Kevin took it personally, as if the criticism was aimed at him and no one else and that Lawrie was calling him a cheat to his face. So he stormed home, saying he would never play for McMenemy again.

"He certainly didn't arrive at the team's hotel with the rest of us for the game at Swansea a couple of evenings later and it was not until about five o'clock that he turned up. He played that night, but the damage was done. He and Lawrie never spoke to each other again until years after Kevin eventually left, to drop down a division with Newcastle United. But if Kevin's flare-up with Lawrie had not happened when it did, I'm sure it would have come sooner or later. Kevin will put his all into something for a few years then he'll want a change, another challenge. He can't seem to settle anywhere for too long and that seems to apply as much to him as a manager as it did during his playing days."

But earlier Keegan, who scored 37 goals for the Saints, had so enjoyed playing with his old mates Channon and Ball that he once remarked that Southampton Football Club should have been re-named Southampton Funball Club. Obviously, that outwardly-genial Geordie, McMenemy, did not always see the funny side of things in the same way as his "bonny lads" did. Consequently, many of the grins and giggles he seemed to enjoy with his team of rascals were manufactured under sufferance and through gritted teeth.

It speaks volumes for the man, though, that he had the courage to try and tame this wild bunch that he had hand-picked himself. There is no more intimidating place on earth than a dressing room or a training ground that is full of young men in the prime of their lives. And he knew that if he gave them an inch they would take a mile, so his balancing act was worth a place in any circus. In a rare serious moment, he once spelled out his aims to Channon by telling him that although it appeared that he was going for the short-term fix when he signed big-name players, the very reverse of that was his true football philosophy. He always had the long-term view in prospect whenever he made a move in the transfer market, he said, because the "old arses" as Channon still called them were the glue he needed to stick the pieces of any future youthful models together in the structure of a side that he believed could reach the highest echelons of the English and even the European game.

If he never quite achieved that dream, he certainly lived up to the traditions of his guardsman past by marching through his career with his own head held high at all times. Naturally, his master-stroke as far as Channon was concerned was to tell him that in this second-time-around journey on which the pair would be travelling together, he would never try and change Channon because he believed that flair and talent should be nourished and not blunted as so many negative "jobsworth" managers were doing at that time. And it was very wise of McMenemy to take that pragmatic view of this prize goalscoring machine.

Because Mick says of himself at that time: "I was just grateful for what the good Lord gave me and got on with it. These were the easy years, I had the pace to go past and get round defenders, coupled with skill on the ball, and on good days I found it a doddle to knock the goals in. The Saints coach, Lew Chatterley, used to say to me: 'How good a player would you be if you trained – the best in the world, or what?' Now, I knew Lew was only trying to wind me up to make me work harder, so my answer was: 'If I'd worked as hard as you wanted me to, I'd have been in the knacker's yard as a 21-year-old.' I'd always been very lazy and never practised my shooting. Most of my football had been purely spontaneous, off-the-cuff stuff. I didn't plan or try to analyse it."

How ironic, then, that in the second half of his life Channon should have turned into such a workaholic! Still, as the old saying goes "There's nowt so queer as folk". Ever the straight talker, Channon adds: "To be honest, I never rated Lawrie too highly when he first came to Southampton. In the beginning I thought he was tactically inept. Still, he was a good listener and he learned something from every good player who ever worked under him. But who am I to talk about the big man that way? I was just a big-headed young git myself in those days.

"So it was just as well that I had to endure a lot of ego-deflation in my short spell at Manchester City. For I now know that humility is good for the soul. That may be the reason why Lawrie and I enjoyed such a happy honeymoon that second time around. And rumour had it that he even went so far as to admit that he was sorry after he broke up our relationship by sticking me on the free transfer list when he eventually thought I was past my sell-by date."

CHAPTER EIGHTEEN
THE ODD TRIO

As football players, Mick Channon, Alan Ball and Kevin Keegan were about as much alike in style as chalk, cheese and a packet of Gary Lineker's potato crisps. If they were horses, Channon would have been the languid, silky- smooth miler, Ball would have been the stoutest stayer in training and Keegan would have been the explosive sprinter. When they joined forces for Southampton they formed one of the most dashing, entertaining trios in the history of club football in this country.

They were all at the back-end of their playing days with highly successful England careers behind them when they came together under that shrewd manager Lawrie McMenemy, a man who, as Channon repeats, "had the psychological skills to suck every last drop of juice out of veteran players and yet kid them that they were enjoying it at the same time". Not that this odd trio needed much kidding. Their mutual love of the racing game, combined with their innate zest for life, had already forged a friendship between them that was to last a lifetime and their uncanny understanding out on the pitch was a natural extension of this bond.

Even a non-gambling man like the Saints boss, McMenemy, was laughingly drawn into their daily, ritualistic, racing game. "They were not exactly subtle about it either," says big Lawrie. "When they turned up for training in the morning and hung binoculars over their dressing-room pegs before spreading that day's edition of the *Sporting Life* across their seats, it didn't take a rocket scientist to work out where they intended to go that afternoon. I had to play an almost daily cat-and-mouse game with them about whether it would be quality or quantity that I got out of them before agreeing to let them go early or not. But when I tell you that, as soon as they were sure I had no objection, Brazil couldn't have looked better on the training pitch than Southampton did then."

McMenemy adds: "The thing that set them apart from other players was that they were, in their different ways, all supreme athletes. And the common bond they had was that they were all very strong personalities. I call players like them the lead violinists of the team. Mick made his name as a striker – for want of a better word – but in my opinion he was unique in that he was a six feet-tall, strong winger who could also fight for the ball just as hard as his two mates. And the fact that I played him out wide a lot of the time meant that he was almost within touching distance of the crowd at The Dell. I know all about Matt Le Tissier after him and Terry Paine before him but Mick still has to be the most revered player in Southampton's history for my money. He was a local boy with charisma and with a great sense of pride in and loyalty to the club. What more could you ask for from a superstar? And don't let anyone kid you that he was just a big country bumpkin. He was always focussed, always knew where he wanted to go in life and brooked no argument about it.

"Looking back, I was wrong to let him go when I did. I should have known he would prove me wrong, of course. And he did, by winning the League Cup Final with Norwich a few years later. I could swear that as I was looking down at him celebrating, from my commentary spot on the TV gantry, I could see him grinning and putting two fingers up at me. It was not the sweetest of partings with Kevin, either, but we all kissed and made up years ago.

"As for the racing game, I did get one over the three of them one day when I took the whole squad for a day at the races and the three experts did their proverbial bollocks on the form horses while I cleaned up with my pin-sticking tactics. OK, so I had to drag my three rascals away from the television at times when the racing was interfering with our preparations but I never saw Mick do anything quite as blatant as I once saw Stan Bowles do. One day when we were playing at Queens Park Rangers, I saw Stan on the phone while the rest were kicking in before the kick-off and it could only have been his bookie he was on the phone to."

Alan Ball pays his mate Mick the ultimate compliment when he says: "As a person, I am proud and privileged to be his friend. As a player he was unique in that he would run and run and run at a defender until the guy cracked and gave in. And without meaning any disrespect to other players, he was virtually doing this on his own at Southampton until Kevin and I arrived to give him a hand. As for the racing, it wasn't very fashionable when us three were at it – not like now when everybody who's anybody in the game wants to own a racehorse. In fact, we were regarded as naughty boys back in the 70s and 80s – scallywags and rascals, if you like. But Mick is no scallywag: he is generous and loyal, the sort of guy anyone would welcome at their side in a crisis. He can be fiery and quick-tempered but he basically loves his fellow human beings as much as any man I know. He adores his family and has a marvellous rapport with his brother, Phil.

"He puts on a hard front as far as the horses are concerned but I happen to know he loves them to death. My greatest pleasure in life now is to stand with him on the gallops at dawn at West Ilsley and listen to him talking aloud to himself about them. He is totally enthralled by his animals and he is fanatical about working out the right races to place them in. I am willing to bet here and now that he will become champion trainer one day – that bloody arthritis of his permitting, of course.

"Mick, Kevin and I have had a million laughs on football grounds and racetracks together and long may the laughs continue. But as owners, both Kevin and I know that when it comes to the serious bit you sit on the fence and let Mick do the talking. You don't tell Mick Channon the trainer to do things, you ask him and then you usually wind up with an earful of swear words for your trouble. He is a good listener but he takes his time to digest what he's hearing. Weirdly enough, though, the memory of the three of us together that still makes me chuckle the most concerns the time Saints were due to play Celtic in the final of a close-season tournament in America.

"Old soldier Lawrie, who was always immaculately dressed himself, had been bending our ears all week long about how smartly the Celtic manager, Billy McNeill, would have his lads turned out for the official reception. He told us that we would more or less face a firing squad if we didn't appear in blazer, shirt and tie for the occasion. But, as I said before, you don't tell Mick Channon to do anything, you ask him. So what does Mick do? He nips out shopping for the three of us and when he comes back he's got three t-shirts with those lurid American ties painted on the front of them. When we stepped out of the lift, and into the banquet looking like that, I thought big Lawrie was going to send us back to the Tower of London on the first plane.

"Little did I dream then, though, that Mick was going to finish up as a guest in Windsor Castle one day. And that he was going to become as respected in racing as he was in football. His biggest asset has been his bravery. He was brave to go into training in the first place. At the time I sensed some of the established trainers thinking: 'What have we got here, then? Is he sure?' And he was brave to take over West Ilsley. And he's brave to go out and buy this big new stud to create an even bigger monster for himself to control."

Kevin Keegan cannot praise Mick Channon highly enough, either. He says simply: "I trust him implicitly and that's the biggest compliment I can pay anybody. The next biggest is that Mick, me and Bally used to kick the crap out of each other in training and never bore the remotest grudge about it. One of the things that set Mick apart was that from when I first knew him in the England Under-23 squad he already had this tremendous knowledge of horses and spent all his spare time with them as if it was his destiny, which we now know it was, of course. He even built his houses around horses and the paddocks were nearly always ready long before the houses."

I suppose it was inevitable that an old Ale House Lad like Channon himself would single out a day's boozing and racing in his beloved Blighty as his favourite anecdote from those happy-go-lucky, three-of-a-kind times.

He recalls: "The three of us were at Brighton races one day when a local landlord we had met there invited us back to his pub after racing. Having a drink with us in the bar was a big, buxom blonde with a green streak in her hair who was well into her fifties, must have weighed at least 14 stones and, as it transpired, was something of a local character. As one drink led to another, she bet Kevin £100 for charity that he couldn't carry her on his shoulders to the next pub, which was about half a mile away.

"This was a mistake. You should never bet against Kevin because he never let anything beat him, especially back in those days when he was in his physical prime. So, sure enough, he picks the old darling up and races full-pelt up quite a steep hill to the other pub and – not content with that – turns straight round with her still on his shoulders and legs it back to the starting point. You can imagine just how startled passers-by must have been, seeing England's most famous footballer performing an antic like this with Alan Ball trailing behind as a referee and me collapsed on the pavement with laughter as Kevin collected his ton for charity.

"One thing was for sure, though, that ride must have hurt the lady more than it hurt Kevin because he was such a strong little devil for his size. And the moment she put her money where her mouth was, as far as he was concerned, she had temporarily forfeited the right to be treated like a lady."

Keegan chuckles when reminded of this anecdote and then smiles: "Mick's got a cheek criticising my behaviour with a lady. I remember being in a box with him at the races one day when he was swearing away like he always does. I happened to know that there was a real lady standing just the other side of him – a genuine member of the aristocracy – so I gave him a dig with my elbow and warned him about it. But then in typical Channon fashion he does no more than turn to the lady and say: 'You'd rather hear language like that than be f---ing deaf, wouldn't you darling?' She just creased up in tears of laughter.

"And that's just another way of my saying that you can't teach Mick anything. He's a natural talent even when it comes to swearing at people and making them think he's not really swearing at all. His secret is that he's so easy with himself. So happy and relaxed with who he is that he's never upset for long. Sure, he flares up, but he always lets the person or persons he's upset with find a dignified way out of the situation.

"I just loved the way Mick played, too. He was a great natural athlete who obviously enjoyed his football. He seemed to give the impression that he was a bit above it all and that it was nowhere near a matter of life and death to him. But underneath that laid-back mask he had a tremendous will to win and a fanatical desire to prove people who doubted him wrong. That was never better illustrated than when he came up to Newcastle to play with me again. We were both near the end of our playing days but the manager, Arthur Cox, and I both felt that Mick was really finished by then. What does the bold Mick do? He goes off and wins the League Cup with Norwich City. I know he played for Manchester City, too, where I am now the manager, of course, but for me Mick will always be synonymous with Southampton. Those red and white stripes used to look as much a part of him as his own pyjamas."

CHAPTER NINETEEN

TRAVELLING

The now almost old-fashioned telephone is still surely the most deadly of instruments even in these high-tech times. Most people learn what destiny next has in store for them when they answer its summons. And so it was with Mick Channon, once again, when he received a phone call at home from Lawrie McMenemy's secretary telling him that the boss would like to see him in his office next morning. Mick remembers that as he replaced the receiver he had one of those weird "for whom the bell tolls" premonitions.

Before reporting to the manager, he shared some black humour with Alan Ball, saying this was probably the prelude to a new contract, but then put in the proviso: "Then again it might be the dreaded free transfer." He was right on the second count when McMenemy said that it was time they parted company again. This time, though, there was to be no move to a glamorous club like Manchester City – only the slippery slope of the "glass mountain" that all veteran players dreaded.

Soccer economics were on a downturn at that particular time and Mick had to accept that, as he was on the wrong side of 30, his wage of nearly £60,000 a year would be enough to buy the Saints three pairs of younger legs. Ever the realist, he knew that Lawrie's suggestion that it was about time he went into management was a euphemism for: "You're over the hill." Mick now says: "I think I was big enough to accept that nothing lasts for ever. And although I might not have liked my sudden departure from The Dell after all those years, or agreed with it, I had to pick myself up and get on with life. It was no good moaning because nobody would listen."

He was shocked and saddened, though, when, like most unemployed men, he suddenly found that people in his profession began avoiding him, through embarrassment. He did, by then, have part-time work as a television panellist during the 1982 World Cup in Spain temporarily to take his mind off his problems before attempting to prove McMenemy wrong about being past his sell-by date.

Although Mick was still steeped in breeding, the idea of training horses for a living had still not even reached the twinkle-in-the-eye stage. But he was to find that there were at least five more good, bad and indifferent years as a full-time footballer still to be travelled on his incredible sporting journey. Mick Channon, the player, was to go on to appear for Newcastle United, Bristol Rovers, Norwich City and Portsmouth as well as travelling to almost all parts of the globe to earn his living the only way he really knew how. For he had already tried and failed at the then ritualistic attempts by footballers to try their luck in business, by teaming up with Peter Osgood for a venture into the meat trade and another crack at sports shop ownership – this time with the equally conventional "dodgy partner" from outside the game.

The first football offer Mick received was to make a guest

appearance for a team in Hong Kong and, later, to take part in a rebel tour of apartheid-ravaged South Africa. As a non-political animal he confesses that he jumped at that one. "Right or wrong," he says, "ten thousand pounds for two weeks' work in the early 1980s was not to be sneezed at by someone who was without a regular job. As it turned out, us rebels were only there for seven days and got paid £6,000 for it. I had been there before to coach black players in the townships so I felt no pangs of guilt for going again. And in between wincing at the way those same players were being treated under the apartheid laws, I must confess I had some great laughs out there."

Every Englishman who has ever kicked a football in that country seems to have run into that legendary extrovert Johnny "Budgie" Byrne, the former West Ham United and England star who was often described as "the British Di Stefano" before being domiciled there. And Channon was no exception. He explains: "Budgie was just like me in that he loved his football and horse racing." Mick was once due to play in Cape Town when he contacted Byrne to invite him to the game, only to be told that Budgie would either be at the game that day or at the local race meeting. Mick reminisces: "I had to laugh because I knew that if Budgie had to choose between seeing me play and a day at the races, the horses would win by a street. So, sure enough, he missed the match. But he turned up at my hotel after the match and he had obviously just enjoyed a cracking day out. I don't mean that he'd won, because he was renowned as one of the world's worst betting men, but I'm sure the booze he had consumed had worked very well as an anaesthetic. We got stuck into the champagne together but he said that he couldn't stay because one of the players in the team he managed was getting married and that he had to make a speech at the reception.

"Several hours and several bottles later, Budgie suggested – or, rather, pleaded – that I should go to the wedding reception with him. Obviously, I knew that old drunk's trick of taking a patsy along to face the wrath of the wife, but plucked up my courage and accompanied him anyway." The rest of this anecdote is predictable but no less amusing for that. Budgie Byrne made a complete balls-up of the speech, Mrs Byrne – after bollocking Budgie – gave Mick a verbal volley and then dragged her husband off to dance. The last Mick saw of Budgie that night was the sight of him lying spark out on the dance floor. Whether it was the drink or his missus that had put him there, Mick did not wait to find out.

That earlier trip to Hong Kong had been even more bizarre. He was accompanied by Saints players David Armstrong and George Lawrence. The three of them were to guest for a well-known team there called Caroline Hill.

It was run by Veronica Chui, a very rich Chinese lady, who owned two clubs in the same Hong Kong league and was attempting to pull off a little scam. She wanted the Saints men to play in the vital last game of the season to prevent one of her teams being relegated. First of all, however, the evening before Mick and his mates were due to play, her other team, which was second in the league, had to beat the second from bottom team in order to avoid Caroline Hill being relegated. It should have been a foregone conclusion. But just to underline that old gambling adage that there is no such thing as a certainty, that team got beaten in what was the turn-up of the season and Mick's match turned out to be meaningless. So Mrs Chui had lost her money, which included air fares, the Saints' wages and no doubt more than a few Hong Kong dollars at the local bookies.

His travels also took Channon to New Zealand and Australia – where as has already been noted – he first met Willie Hastings-Bass. Another racing enthusiast he teamed up with whilst playing for Newcastle Raiders in Australia was Irishman Chris Docherty, who had been out there since he was a small boy. The pair went racing together in all parts of that vast country and they shared the driving for an 11-hour journey from Sydney to Brisbane to attend a prestigious $100,000 sprint race. They stayed on the Gold Coast, just outside Brisbane, on the way up but torrential rain flooded the roads and they stayed an extra day before driving back by a different inland route. "Chris seemed to know all about every horse in Australia and, like practically every Aussie punter I ever met, he had bags of bottle when it came to putting his money down."

The most unlikely of Mick's travelling tales is the one in which he and dear old strait-laced Trevor Brooking became partners. He recalls: "Trevor and me found ourselves in New Zealand together. We used to do a double act as guest after-dinner speakers. Trevor, being Trevor, played the straight man, of course, whilst I was the naughty boy telling all the blue jokes."

CHAPTER TWENTY

THE GLASS MOUNTAIN

The dreaded glass mountain that Mick Channon and other veteran players dreaded began to loom inescapably into view for him after he was discarded by his beloved Saints in 1982. The severance of his ties with the club that had provided him with a living and a purpose in life left him between a rock and a hard place.

The rock was the lifelong, burning ambition for personal fulfilment that still smouldered within him. The hard place was the low level of realistic expectations he was left with to keep that flame burning. And just to make the journey even more perilous, that arch-liar, the late and largely unlamented pension robber, Sir Robert Maxwell, also chose to throw in a banana skin. As chairman of Oxford United, Maxwell cynically took the opportunity of staging a mock interview with Mick to offer him the job of manager of his Second Division team; a job that Mick believes Maxwell had no intention of giving him.

"He was just using my name for cheap publicity," recalls Mick.

"The old devil even had pressmen making notes and photographers taking pictures of our meeting." The harsh fact was that Mick's name still meant something in terms of celebrity because of his temporary high profile as a television football panellist. But long term, he was fast becoming just another seen-it-done-it-bought-the-T-shirt old footballer, who just happened to breed and own a few horses as a hobby. He himself puts it this way: "Whether clubs were frightened of me because of my outspoken views on television, or perhaps they thought I'd want too much money, I don't know. All I can say is that nobody else asked me to do a job for them and it looked as though I was out on my ear."

All that was left career-wise was the charity of the old pals' network. And that was certainly not the strongest of weapons in the insecure dog-eat-dog world of professional football.

First up with an attempted rescue was Kevin Keegan. Unbeknown to Mick, Keegan arranged for his pal to try his luck as a part-timer with Newcastle, that sleeping giant, for whom he was now plying his trade. But with just four Second Division appearances and with only one goal to his credit, Mick soon found himself back in the shit – shovelling shit again back home with his horses.

Next up was Mick's old Ale House mate, big John McGrath, who was then managing Port Vale. But the two of them got only as far as sharing a few "good-old-days" anecdotes. Bobby Gould was next in the frame, when he put up a case to lure Mick down to Bristol. He was convinced that, with a little bit of help from his old friend, he could get Rovers promoted from the Third Division and Mick agreed to go there on a part-time basis, training one day a week. Rovers turned out to be the one and only club for which Channon never scored and it took him and Gould only four matches to realise that one day a week was definitely not enough physical preparation for professional football. But, by way of compensation, Bobby got his club some short-lived publicity out of the brief liaison.

All Mick got was that hellish, washed-up feeling that only people who have been there can truly understand. So it was more with the intention of drowning his sorrows rather than celebrating the fact that it was Christmas week that he accepted an invitation to go racing with Alan Ball at Fontwell Park one day in late December of that fateful year of 1982. With Bally was another racing nut and another old England team-mate in the muscular shape of goalkeeper Peter Shilton, who had recently joined Southampton himself.

As the drink flowed, Mick took his bad mood out on his mates and started reminding Peter that, during their time together in the England squad, the big keeper was such a boring, long-winded card player that the rest of the team called him "Mogadon", after the sleeping tablets. Shilton retaliated with some tough-love talk that had the same life-changing effect on Mick as the training-ground bollocking he had taken from Peter Osgood years earlier. As if to make a point that he was later going to prove himself by playing on well into his forties, "Shilts" called Channon a lazy git and, worse, then told him that he should give the shit-shovelling a rest for a while and get back into training every day.

Mick says: "I brooded on the truth of what Peter had said all next day. I knew I was too heavy and that, without the discipline of regular training, I would be getting heavier by the day. I was just thinking that the only place I was headed for was the scrapheap, then – wouldn't you know it – the phone rang with an offer for me to go up to Norwich to talk to their manager, Ken Brown, the next morning. The fact that the next day was Christmas Eve and that my car was off the road following a crash did not deter me one bit. I had that last-chance saloon feeling deep inside me and responded to it by hiring a Mini and squeezing my overweight frame into it for the long journey. It seemed to take forever. The roads were jammed with carloads of Christmas shoppers. And I had to endure the laborious long haul along the A11 before they built the motorway. But that gave me plenty of time to resolve that if the Canaries were about to offer me a return to the First Division big-time, I was going to snatch their claws off.

"I say 'big time' but Norwich were bottom of the League and I was needed to play on Boxing Day at Ipswich because strikers John Deehan and Keith Bertschin were out through injury and suspension. So there I was being thrown back straight into the red–hot East Anglian derby, which we won 3-2. I didn't score in that game but I put matters right the very next day when I got the winner in a 1-0 victory over Luton. We negotiated a month-on–month rolling contract and I went back into serious daily training and played regularly for Norwich for the next two and a half years.

"To be fair to Ken Brown, when he took me to meet his chairman, Sir Arthur South, he told me: 'If it wasn't for the chairman, you wouldn't be here.' We managed to finish out of trouble halfway up the table that season and when, later, we went to Wembley to play in the League Cup Final and I went up to collect my Milk Cup winner's medal, I don't know who was happier, me, Sir Arthur or my son Michael."

Michael Channon junior was ten years old when his dad came up with the innovative idea of inviting him on to the Norwich bench for that Sunday afternoon Milk Cup Final kick-off against Sunderland. Young Michael was smuggled into the ground dressed as a mascot in his Canaries tracksuit and even did a lap of honour afterwards with his old man and his victorious team-mates after their 1-0 triumph. Not to be outdone, Mick's daughter Nicola, who was then 13, had her hair sprayed in Norwich's green and yellow colours. "To anyone else she would have looked like an outrageous punk; to my wife Jane and me, she was gorgeous," purrs Mick. "I will always love Ken Brown for allowing my lad to have that unique experience and I was lucky in that as I was at the veteran stage by then, no one else in the team had a grown-up son so I wasn't stepping on anyone else's toes or denying anyone else a privilege." Although Mick and Jane had joined together to make the League Cup Final fun for their children, the couple's marriage had, by then, run its course although Mick and Jane remained good friends – and still are.

Sadly for Norwich, though, that season ended with tears of despair as well as tears of joy, when they were relegated. And, even more sadly for Channon, this financial disaster for the club meant that after two and a half years he had to wave goodbye to what he describes as "my days of sanctuary with my lovely village green team".

One of the more obvious reasons why Mick was so happy at Norwich was that he met his present wife Jill while he was playing for the Canaries and they settled down to plan a life together. He says, incidentally, that he also had an excellent relationship with the crowd at Carrow Road. But being the reckless character that he was, he nearly ruined all of that before it had even got started. Now, Mick is the first to admit that when those excitable juices flow through his veins he is capable of having a row with himself in an otherwise empty phone box.

The then Norwich coach, Mel Machin, is a man Mick was to come to admire more than any other and Mick says unhesitatingly: "He was the best coach I ever played under and if I owned a football club instead of racehorses, Mel would be the first man I would want to employ to prepare the team for a game and then get the maximum out of them. But I almost blew away our relationship with my bad temper." The two men had an almighty bust-up when the club had a bad result in an FA Cup tie at Derby County. At that time Derby were struggling near the bottom of the Second Divison so their victory over First Division Norwich represented a giant-killing.

Mick still claims that the then Derby winger, John Robertson, who had starred for Nottingham Forest and Scotland, and is now Martin O'Neill's assistant at Celtic, dived in the box and conned the referee into giving his team a penalty. (So there's proof, if it were needed, that there is nothing new under the sun and that controversy over suspected penalty-box diving was not imported to the English League by Tottenham Hotspur's German star Jurgen Klinsmann, as so many younger soccer fans seem to think these days.) According to Mick, Mel bottled up his feeling over that 2-1 defeat until shortly before they were due to kick off against West Ham United a week later.

"In the team talk, he laid into us big time and said that all the Norwich fans were absolutely disgusted with us for letting them down so badly. Now, I knew plenty of those fans myself, who happened to share my opinion that we were just unlucky at Derby and when I said so it sparked off a massive stand-up row between us," Mick recalls. "The younger lads did not know where to put themselves as we both clenched our fists and called each other every name we could think of. Even the manager, Ken Brown, did not seem able to step in and stop it.

"It turned out to be the biggest row I'd ever had with anyone in football. But we then went out and beat the Hammers 1–0. Yet, at the end, when we came back into the dressing room, I could see that Mel was still sulking. Now, I used to shoot off straight after games in order to get back home to the horses and unless there was a midweek game I'd have a long weekend before driving back to Norwich. So it wasn't until the end of the next week that I saw Mel again and he told me that he had been shaking all that weekend and that he wanted to get me sacked there and then. But eventually we shook hands, made up and went all the way to Wembley together."

As a happier postscript to what he describes as the peace and tranquillity of those East Anglian years, Mick feels the need to mention that when he stayed overnight at Norwich, it was at a charming little hotel called "Oaklands". He reminisces: "The owner, George Dack, loved horse racing almost as much as me but unfortunately I kept tipping him losers. Sorry about that, George."

CHAPTER TWENTY-ONE

BACK WITH BALLY

Amazingly for a front-runner, Mick Channon still had one "last hurrah" left in him even though he was now only a couple of years off the age of 40. Predictably enough, this was with Alan Ball, who was by now managing Portsmouth in the Second Division. According to Mick, his old mate had put together a "dirty dozen" or so rejects and ne'er-do-wells that nobody else wanted because of their reputations as boozers, barrack-room lawyers and the like. "It was just like the old Ale House days at Southampton; as if I'd come full circle," he recalls.

Best mates Channon and Ball never wanted to talk soccer-shop together so before Mick joined Portsmouth, their still-frequent telephone conversations nearly always centred on horse racing. So, naturally enough, on the July morning that Alan rang Mick it happened to be the Monday following Glorious Goodwood and Mick was expecting Bally to discuss the shit-cart of a racing card that day, which always followed this marvellous historic meeting as surely as it used to follow the Lord Mayor's

Show down the centuries. "But Bally just said to me," remembers Mick, " 'Get your arse down here. The chairman wants to see you so you might as well come and join us for a month.' "

Ball explained that he had been trying to buy people on permanent transfer but clubs were asking silly money for people who couldn't tie Channon's laces – old as he then was. Naturally, Mick was flattered by his mate's little bit of flannel, but he admitted that this was a situation that he had always wanted to try to avoid. He explains: "Bally was my best mate and I didn't want anything to threaten that relationship, least of all a football club – any bloody football club. There were enough nasty-minded people around who would only be too ready to start spreading rumours that if I joined Pompey in any capacity, I was going after Bally's job.

"There was no need to tell Alan that, as he would have trusted me with his life, so I went down to see his chairman, John Deacon, and I was soon back in business yet again. The discussions went so well that I was asked to sign for a full season, which I duly did. I was slightly dubious about it because I didn't want to put Bally in an embarrassing position if it turned out that I couldn't cut the mustard any more and he had to ask me to play in the reserves. He knew that I would never allow myself to finish my playing days in anyone's reserve team, not even his, so he just laughed in my face when I said I was worried."

Well, Bally's bunch of talented discards, with Channon up front, soon went storming up to the top of the table and Mick describes their tactics, or the lack of them, this way: "Every one of those Pompey lads was a fierce competitor who would hurl himself into the thick of a match quite blindly at times. But to harness all that raw and often neglected talent and passion was a massive job for Bally. All they wanted to do was win. They didn't know or care how to play occasionally for a draw, and that cost them promotion.

"They all trained and worked hard as well as playing hard on and off the pitch, but when things went wrong they wanted to fight the world instead of playing it tight. But it gave me the greatest of pleasure to see them do it right for Bally the very next season when they finally clinched that precious First Division spot for him by finishing second to Derby County." Channon was not around to share in that triumph, however. For by then this old warhorse had finally retired from the fray for good to nurse his wounds and mull over his future.

Little did he know then what wounds and what a future they would turn out to be.

In common with dozens of his mates, he still suffers the physical infirmities of that 1970s generation who went down in medical history as victims of the cortisone scandal. Cortisone was the pain-killing drug that has since been banned and has blighted the lives of too many former stars to be named here.

It was the disgusting policy of most clubs then to play unfit players over and over again by sticking so many cortisone injections into their injuries that many of them must have finished up with legs looking like dartboards.

Mick's most memorable recollection of this terrible trend was when his foot was shot full of the deadly liquid so that his bruised big-toe nail could be ripped off in the White Hart Lane dressing room before playing in a match for Southampton at Tottenham Hotspur. And he went on to play for 70 of the 90 minutes before the pain returned and it became unbearable. Unlike dozens more of his half-crippled mates who have suffered the long-term effects of those constant football injuries, Channon has, of course, gone on to be one of life's winners despite having to hobble about and pop pills in his constant daily battle against arthritis. And it was during the last part of his spell at Portsmouth that the idea finally settled in his mind that he must somehow try to get a living out of his other love – racing.

"I was in a worse state mile-wise than so many of the old cars I had burned out travelling the length and breadth of the country as a part-timer," he says. "I knew it was time to settle down at last, but like the old joke says: 'I had to settle up first.' And as settling up usually means starting at the bottom again and working your way up that is what, after much soul-searching, he decided to do. Towards the end of his playing days at Pompey, he began jokingly telling anyone who wanted to know that he was now a professional racing man who played football for fun. This was the time when another colourful and prolific goalscoring player who gloried in the nickname "The Mighty Quinn" joined Portsmouth and fell under Channon's spell.

Mick Quinn was to finish up with more than 230 goals in his 512 League games and although he joined Portsmouth midway through his career, he freely admits that Channon helped Ball to knock some of the rougher edges off his rough and ready game. They did this to the extent that the big Liverpudlian went on to score more than 50 goals for the club. Quinn remembers: "Us younger players had a little drinking and gambling clique and we used to slope down to the bookies and the boozer most days after training. I was in awe of Mick then; he would stroll in for training in his cloth cap, his wellies covered with horse shit and with *The Sporting Life* tucked under his arm. He would take the piss out of the other lads by shouting 'Mornin' reserves' as if he could read Bally's mind as to who and who would not be getting picked for the first team that week.

"This became such a ritual that he and Alan eventually went shares in a horse together and named it 'Mornin Reserves'. Mick had all the self-confidence you would expect from a great international star. But he was never openly arrogant. Naturally, he had slowed down by the time I played with him but although he

PRESIDENT-
THE RIGHT HON. EARL CADOGAN.

Telephone,
FULHAM 5545.

Telegrams.
CHELSTAM, LONDON. S.W.6.

Stamford Bridge Grounds,
Fulham Road,
London, S.W.6

Secretary.
J. BATTERSBY.

2nd March 1964.

Mr. M. Channon,
2 Whatcombe Brow,
Orcheston,
SALISBURY.

Dear Michael,

    A Schoolmaster friend of this club has sent us
a strong recommendation that you are a very promising young
Footballer.   In order that we may have your full background,
would you please fill in the enclosed Youth form and return
for further consideration?

    Our Youth scheme has been highly successful,
and if a boy has the ability and determination to become
a first class player, we do all we can to foster that spirit.

    Could we please ask that you do not sign for any
club until we have had a chance of assessing your potentiality,
and also, if you could let me have the name and address of
your Secretary of School or Club outside School, this would
enable us to make the proper approach.

    With thanks in anticipation and best wishes
for your ultimate success,

Yours sincerely,

L A Beaford

Chief Representative.

A letter from Chelsea F.C. – Michael was beginning to interest several clubs by 1964
(courtesy of Mrs Betty Channon).

Mick's not sure what's making Alf Ramsey and Bobby Moore smile at England training, November 1966 (© Daily Mirror).

October 1973: the look says it all. Mick Channon, Tony Currie and Mick Mills leave the field drained and dejected after somehow failing to defeat Poland in that crucial World Cup qualifier (© London Photo Agency).

A game of cribbage with England team-mates Kevin Keegan, Alan Ball and David Johnson, 1975 (© Daily Mirror).

Mesmerising the Manchester United defence in the 1976 FA Cup final (© Daily Mirror).

With first wife Jane and children Nicky and Michael junior, celebrating Southampton's FA Cup final triumph over Manchester United in 1976 (© Southern Newspapers Ltd).

Letting The Dell faithful get a glimpse of that famous old trophy (© Daily Mirror).

Another goal for his beloved Saints, and there's that trademark windmill celebration (© MSI).

Elegantly stroking the ball forward against Arsenal, August 1980 (© MSI).

With his son Michael junior, celebrating Norwich's League Cup success at Wembley in 1985 (© Universal Pictorial Press).

Devising plans for Ascot's Shergar Cup with old pal Kevin Keegan, August 2000 (© Mike King).

Demonstrating that the skill never leaves you to fellow trainers Saeed Bin Suroor, Ben Hanbury and David Elsworth at Ascot, 1998 (© Independent).

Making plans in his office at the West Ilsley stables that have turned out so many winners over the years (© Gerry Cranham).

The daily ritual of scrutinising his string of horses as they make their way to the gallops (© Gerry Cranham).

Enjoying an evening with [from left to right] the late Neil Crook, George Cohen, Colin Ingleby-McKenzie and Alan Ball (© The Country Gentlemen's Association).

Mick with his six-month-old grandson, Archie, at Goodwood racecourse, 12 September 2003, the day Mick reached the 100-winner mark for the season (courtesy of Nicky Channon).

Never happier than when working in his yard (© Gerry Cranham).

Mick with wife Jill and children Jack and India (courtesy of Mrs Betty Channon).

was always full of light-hearted banter, he would whip the rest of us to death with his tongue whenever he thought we deserved it. And I've seen that old cloth cap of his come flying off on the gallops when he is upset. But I had to wait a few years for this memorable sight. For when I eventually finished playing myself and Mick had gone into full-time training, I begged him to give me a job in his yard and teach me the ins and outs of the training game.

"The language he used, to try and put me off, beggared description even for someone who could swear like me. But after he had bollocked me for a being a crazy so and so, he took me on and I learned to shovel shit with the best of 'em. By then, I had already taken a quarter share in one of his syndicates for a two-year-old colt called Land Sun. Like a lot of the Pompey players back then, he was a moody git and would pull himself up at times.

"But I'll never forget the day he won for the first time at Woverhampton races. Mick was with me and so were dear old Frank Worthington and Frannie Lee, who was himself a fully-fledged trainer by then. As we roared our lad home, I heard one of the more toffee-nosed trainers' disparaging remark to his tweed-and-corduroy companion: 'It seems you have to be a footballer to be rich enough to own a racehorse these days.' I just thought: 'Fuck him. I'm sure Mick felt the same way.' "

CHAPTER TWENTY-TWO

HALF-TIME

The days of being able to indulge in the luxury of telling people to go and fuck themselves in the manner that big, brash Quinn had surmised that Mick would do, were actually long gone for Mick. He knew that the first half of his life had just been played out in injury time to such an extent that at Portsmouth he was forced to laugh away the agony of the dying of the athletic light by boasting that he was still the highest-paid player in the land because he could only usually manage the first 45 minutes of a match before his legs gave out and his mate Bally had to substitute him.

So after much sucking at a symbolic half-time lemon, he had decided that if he wanted to have a life after football, diplomacy and discretion would have to take precedence over what, in his headstrong youth, he had once regarded as outspoken valour. He was past the halfway stage of the biblical three score years and ten and he not only had an irrecoverable career behind him but sadly, a marriage too. He and his first wife, Jane, were the same age and had been teenage sweethearts. They had both been 23 when they had wed and they had started married life in a semi-detached house in a Southampton suburb. Local girl Jane was a hairdresser and this gave Mick an early opportunity to try his luck in business when he bought a hairdressing shop near The Dell for Jane. His brother, Phil, helped her run it.

Their two children, Nicky and Michael junior, were born in 1972 and 1974 respectively and when Nicky was six months old they bought a property called Lower Chase Farm at Swanmore, where Cathy Jane and another three broodmares were installed in the adjoining stable. Brother Phil, who was rapidly turning into a jack-of-all-trades, helped Mick there too.

Jane looks back on that time as the happiest of her life. She recalls: "All the wives of the Saints players got on really well together. But there were no such things as luxury boxes or players' lounges in those days. All we had as a meeting point on match days was a tiny little cubbyhole of a room that was allocated to us for our half-time cup of tea. We loved getting together there for a good gossip and we used to socialise together too, with the odd meal in a restaurant, but we had nothing as remotely glamorous as the modern-day lifestyles of Victoria Beckham and the rest of today's football wives."

What Jane did have, however, was a husband who was obsessed with horses. She explains: "Mick never ever talked football at home – only horses. No doubt he discussed the game with his mates but at home all his spare time was taken up tending the horses or burying his head in breeding books. Not that I minded too much because his enthusiasm was so infectious that his brother Phil and I were eventually as wrapped up in them as he was. And as for our children, their greatest thrill in life when they were small was to be allowed to see foals being born. We even had to wake them up in the middle of the night when one was due so that they could stand in their dressing gowns and wellies watching, wide-eyed, as either Cathy Jane or one of her pals gave birth."

But all this was to change when Mick was transferred to Manchester City. And Jane confirms that, as Mick has already described, these were undoubtedly the two most frustrating years of his life. "What with his injury and his lack of form, he almost forgot about his horses and started bringing his football worries home for the first time in his life," she says. "When Mick moved to Manchester City we bought a detached house in Altrincham, Cheshire, where most of the other Manchester-based players lived. But Mick found he was really missing his horses and so, whenever he could, he took the opportunity of blasting up and down the motorway to visit them at Lower Chase Farm."

Another thing Mick Channon loved in his playing heyday was being a man of the people and mixing socially with the fans whenever he had the chance. And nowhere was he happier doing this than at his beloved Southampton. "We had only moved back to Southampton for a few weeks when I knew he was the old, happy-go-lucky Mick again," adds Jane. "That was when he started going to the local occasionally to have a game of crib with some of the old chaps there. By then, Mick had made the unshakeable decision that the way he was going to get most out of his life was by concentrating on his horses as much as on his football.

"So," says Jane, "towards the end of our stay up north, we decided to sell Lower Chase Farm and bought a few acres of land at Fair Oak in Hampshire, midway between Eastleigh and Winchester, where Phil looked after the horses while we waited for our brand new house to be built, which we named Jamesmead after one of Mick's horses. That turned into a fully-fledged stud farm. Unfortunately, we split up while we were at Jamesmead. So

I bought a house in Southampton for me and the children and Mick bought a flat.

"We later divorced, but we have always been the best of friends since.You couldn't make an enemy out of Mick even if you wanted to – he's just too nice a guy for that.We just grew away from each other as husband and wife, though. Although we divorced and Phil got married and had a family himself, Phil and I learned how to foal the horses between us. We still spent a lot of our time at Jamesmead and so did Mick. Even after Mick had gone to Norwich he used to spend every other weekend at Jamesmead to see the children and the horses, of course."

It was whilst Mick and Jane and their two young children were living at Jamesmead that they formed a friendship with a family who did more than anyone to change Mick's life. John Baker, who is now deceased, and his sons Trevor and Rodney ran a racing stable down in Devon, which the Channons would visit on social calls. Jane explains: "We had a close friend in Hampshire called Michael Packenham, who was our young Michael's godfather. The Packenhams moved down to Devon and became friendly with the Bakers.We used to go and visit them down there and it wasn't long before Mick and the Bakers became close friends, too."

John Baker agreed to train a horse called Man On The Run, which Mick and Kevin Keegan owned jointly and that turned out to be a winner and a very consistent and genuine horse into the bargain. Mick also sent the syndicate-owned Spark Off to the Bakers. Spark Off was, of course, the hurdler that landed that huge Channon betting coup at a New Year's Day jumps meeting at Devon and Exeter. More significantly, it was the Bakers to whom Mick turned when he decided to try his luck at training.

That decision took a long time coming. "I made it out of desperation as much as anything," Mick remembers. "This had been the worst period of my life – never mind anything as colourful as a glass mountain, it felt more like the scrapheap that I was on. For the first time, I felt old – really old. And I slumped into self-pity. What with my family splitting up and my legs and feet getting so sore that I was struggling to get out of bed in the morning, I started to think: 'No one wants you when you're old; no one wants anyone when they're old.' Looking back, I realised that when I bought Cathy Jane, I had not had the slightest idea of becoming a trainer."

But some of the people that knew him best were encouraging Mick not just to dream the impossible dream of becoming a trainer himself but to actually go out and live it. He had previously thought that buying, selling and breeding horses would be more than enough to satisfy him. So much so that he set up the Mick Channon Bloodstock business that has continued to thrive until this day. But his innate competitive nature kept nagging at him and would never let him rest until he tried what his friends suggested and actually went out to emulate what his old England playmate, Frannie Lee, had done with his horses and that was to "train the buggers myself".

Mick adds: "Slowly, I started to agree with this positive advice I was being given. I thought 'I'm too good for the scrapheap. I'm too competitive to pack up being a professional sportsman completely.' " And being a man who had always known that actions spoke louder than words for him, he knew he would have to try and get a licence from the Jockey Club as soon as possible. And as he had neither experience, a title, a double-barrelled name nor had been an officer in the Guards, he was just going to have to shovel shit for somebody else first.

So he made the momentous, life-changing decision to go not only to Devon as unpaid assistant trainer to John Baker but to go and live with the man as well.

All this meant waving goodbye to the carefree, punting days of his youth. "My gambling had already turned into buying mares, putting them in foal and spending money on nomination fees. And if I was going to train, too, I sure as hell couldn't spend all day running up and down to the bookies," he grins.

Not that his previous involvement with the gee-gees had lacked excitement or tension. He still trembles with the excitement of it all when he recalls: "We broke horses and got them ready for racing on the farm. At least 40 young horses went through my hands at my little studs, the most notable being Jamesmead and that great chaser Ghofar, who was out of my Cup-final mare, Royale Final, of course. And old Ghofar went on to win the Hennessy Gold Cup after I sold him to my old mate, David Elsworth, who later sold him on to Lord Oaksey.

"I wasn't stupid, though. I made sure I was strictly a one-man band in business." The thought of going into partnership with anyone was anathema to him. For like so many of his professional playing contemporaries, he had already had his fingers burnt at that game. "The hairdressers was a success because I kept that in the family," says Mick, "but when I got involved in a sports shop with a couple of local lads, one of them turned out to be a rip-off merchant. I could tell it was going to go tits-up almost from day one.

"After this I made sure that the only people I got involved with to help me were the very best in their field — the best solicitor, the best accountant, the best secretary and so on. As for the horses, jockeys and stable staff, that was just a case of talent spotting on my part. Peter Osgood and I did invest in a venture with a smashing old bloke Stan Hensham, though. Stan was a wholesale butcher selling from his farm. He was straight as a die. He's dead now, bless him, but it was Stan who sold me the land for my first stud.

"I had always been more comfortable with country folk like

Stan and some of his pals were among my first owners. That's why I was happy to go down to Devon with the Bakers." Little did he know then, though, that he would go on to do business with owners who would include corporate managers, millionaires, actors and even English and Arab royalty.

CHAPTER TWENTY-THREE

DEVON

The Bakers still regard Mick as "family". Trevor, who is now a chicken farmer, was the first of the Baker boys to pal up with Mick. He explains: "We first became friends through our mutual love of shooting. Michael Packenham brought Mick to a pheasant shoot at Mapperton Manor in Dorset one day and Mick was hooked." But this was one of the very few sporting talents that did not come so naturally to Channon. "He was dead keen," admits Trevor, but then he laughs and adds: "He definitely was not a world-class marksman, though. His strike rate was nothing like as good as it was on the soccer field."

It was not long before Mick decided to place one of the horses he and his various syndicates owned by now with Trevor's father John and brother Rodney, who ran the family's small racing stable at Shillingford in North Devon. "Unfortunately, it was such a useless animal that I can't even remember its name or its sex," says Rodney. "But then, of course, he sent us Man On The Run and Spark Off and that was the beginning of our serious relationship."

When Mick decided to go down to live with the Bakers to learn the training business inside out, they had 14 boxes at their tiny Shillingford base and he brought six two-year-olds with him, swelling the number of inhabitants to 20. And as the stable grew, they moved to Stoodleigh, where Rodney still trains a few of Mick's horses. "They are more or less lodgers now," explains Rodney, because he is so full up at West Ilsley."

At this crossroads in his life, Channon decided to live with John Baker for five nights a week after John's wife died. Rodney explains: "My wife and I moved out into a caravan for a while until dad died. My father and Mick had the utmost respect for each other and it is no exaggeration to say he treated him like a son and that Trevor and I regarded him as a brother.

"He turned out to be grand company for dad, who would have had to live alone otherwise. Mind you, dad said he couldn't get him to help with the washing-up for love nor money although he did do his share of the cooking. But he couldn't wait to get home to his children and his horses at the weekends. The one virtue above all others that Mick had to learn to become the trainer he is today was patience. He used to fly off the handle if he didn't get his own way at times, but I told him that would get him nowhere and he did learn eventually, bless him. But then our way of life and the slower way we had of doing things couldn't have been more different from the hurly-burly world of football that he was brought up in. He liked to run his horses as often as possible. He used to say: 'I worked bloody hard at football; why shouldn't they work hard, too? It will do them good.'

"He had this saying that he picked up from Richard Hannon: 'They won't earn their keep stuck in the stable all day, admiring the view.' And that's a policy he still pursues today, of course. As everyone in racing now knows, Mick has a particular knack of spotting and preparing two-year-olds, especially two-year-old fillies. He just seems to have an eye for picking them out at the sales and then bringing them to fruition.

"Maybe they respond to his generous nature. He is certainly the most generous friend I have ever had. One day at Worcester races he backed a few winners. The next thing you know is that he's got a wad of notes in his hand. He gives me the lot and says: "Buy yourself a cup of tea, Rodney. When I counted it up later it came to more than £1,000. But in those days, when he was still a gambler, you could find him at the races the next week with just a £50 note and a credit card to hand.

"Another example of his generosity came later when he had moved up, up and away. A local village amateur football team got me to ask Mick to draw the raffle at their annual 'do'. They were so small-time that the entire population of the village couldn't have been more than 2,000 people. Yet Mick drove three hours each way from his home to oblige."

It was while he was with the Bakers that Channon trained his very first, hands-on winner. But as he was still unlicensed he had to run it under the Bakers' training banner. The horse's name was Super Zoom and it won a three-horse race on the rainy evening of 21 July 1988 at Chepstow Racecourse, which, at a distance of 80 miles, was the nearest track to the Bakers' stable. Super Zoom started at the exorbitant odds of 33 to 1 and it was, in its own way, as fantastic an achievement for Mick as scoring a hat-trick in a World Cup Final would have been. The thrill of that triumph still has Rodney Baker chuckling all these years later. But as if to prove that Mick Channon and unlikely sporting success will always be bedfellows, he reminds me that they pulled off a similar 33 to 1 coup as recently as 11 June 2002.

The winning venue was Salisbury, and this time they had 18 other horses to beat in an amateur riders' handicap. And this time the winning credentials read: trainer R J Baker; owner M R Channon. In contrast, by this time my own life consisted of rock bottom after rock bottom. Chronic alcoholism had reduced me to the state where I begged, borrowed and stole money so that I could blow what was left of my brains out on booze. It was around this time that I began noticing Mick Channon's rise through the racing ranks and if I was in any way jealous of the way he was getting his life together so successfully, I wasn't showing it because, like most other alcoholics, I still possessed such a wilful ego that I could lie in the gutter looking down at the people passing by.

Incidentally, don't let anyone tell you that alcoholics have about as much willpower as a melting snowflake because the reverse is true. Sadly – and this is what ruins so many potential recoveries – we have the willpower of tigers in that when we are "using", nothing will prevent us from finding the means of getting a drink.

And it was precisely this compulsion that propelled me down to David Elsworth's stable for my Christmas earner in 1991 to do a freelance piece for *The Daily Star* on that equine superstar Desert Orchid. I had dreamed up a stunt of sticking a Santa Claus hat on the fabulous, grey steeplechaser, Dessie, who was due to compete in his favourite race, the King George, at Kempton Park on Boxing Day.

And David was so delighted with the Father Christmas photograph I had arranged that, I was told, he turned it into a Christmas card. David also tipped up one of his horses for me to share with my down-and-out mates for our Christmas drink money but typically the going changed overnight, the horse got beaten, we all did our 'bollocks' on it and didn't have a penny on when it won next time out.

By now, I had got it into my booze-warped brain that Mick was living the proverbial life of Riley, poncing about in the owners' and trainers' bar at the races all day when, in fact, he was putting me to shame. I remembered that "Up at Six to Feed the Chicks" had been his favourite party piece of a song in those good old bad old days of yore but in fact he was now having to get up even before the cockerels began their dastardly dawn chorus. Not only that but the simple act of getting out of bed was becoming increasingly painful for him as arthritis began gnawing ever deeper into his cortisone-damaged bones.

CHAPTER TWENTY-FOUR
LICENCE

A day at the races can be glamorous and glorious for the average punter. For a trainer on the bottom rung of the ladder, as Mick Channon was when he began operating in the late 1980s, it is a different matter. The words of encouragement that you fantasised would help propel your horse to the head of a field of Flat-race runners and riders soon get stuck in your throat as your pride and joy falls away behind the others as if it were a broken bead rolling away from a child's colourful necklace. Far from being able to laud it as conquering hero at National Hunt meetings, more often than not you watch thoroughly depressed as your mud-spattered "fella" returns to the unsaddling enclosure looking like a straggler from Napoleon's depleted cavalry on the retreat from Moscow.

Mick's nearest and dearest simply thought he was mad to risk what was left of his modest football nest egg on such a perilous way of life but he was determined to do so. After a year of invaluable tuition from the Bakers down in Devon, Mick decided to join up with an established trainer in Ken Cunningham-Brown, a move that ill-informed cynics might have asserted meant he had one eye on winning his trainer's licence from the Jockey Club's idiosyncratic licensing board and the other on making life as a trainer easier on himself through association with Ken's conveniently double-barrelled surname. The truth was that it was simply for geographical reasons that headstrong Mick made the move.

Cunningham-Brown had a yard called Danebury Place in Stockbridge, which happened to be located right in Mick's own backyard at Salisbury. And what a romantic racing spot it turned out to be. Ken had installed an all-weather track around what is still left of the old grandstand at Stockbridge Races, a historic course that went out of existence just after the First World War. And the stable's list of illustrious old-time trainers included Lester Piggott's great-grandfather.

Another truth behind Mick's change of plans – and this was a much more painful one – was that his first application for a licence was turned down under such ironic circumstances that the situation would have been laughable had it not had such serious consequences not long afterwards.

On the day Channon was called before the licensing committee to stake his claim there were only two applicants being interviewed – he and an ex-rider named Dermot Browne. And Mick remembers: "I feared the worst when one of the committee asked me if I rode out regularly when one look at my heavyweight, 15-stone body should have answered that ludicrous question."

The son of a Classic-winning trainer, Browne once threatened to outstrip even his father's achievements when he became champion amateur jump jockey. So it was no great shock that when the two interviews were over, it was Browne who came out to do a lap of honour as the successful applicant and the failed ex-footballer Channon who had his head in his chest. But as a fully-fledged Lambourn-based trainer, Browne went on to be found guilty by the Jockey Club of ordering a jockey to pull a horse at Leicester and selling inside information to a bookmaker. As a result he was banned from racing for ten years." And he has since admitted doping a further 23 horses for on-the-run cocaine-trafficker Brian Wright and has been warned off for 20 more years.

Although he felt like crying at the time, the irrepressible Channon is able now to manage a rueful smile at the ludicrous mess the Jockey Club unwittingly made of its licensing business on that fateful day. His long-time racing pal, ace trainer David Elsworth, smiles about it too, when he recalls: "Just before Mick had to go up for that interview, he and I were travelling to the sales together when we happened to see one of the Jockey Club licensing officers at a service station.

"Now I had been in a spot of bother with the authorities myself at that time and I wasn't flavour of the month with them so I tried to warn Mick that, to be on the safe side, he should avoid letting himself be seen in my company by this man. But Mick being Mick, just said "bollocks" to that and he let us both be seen together as bold as brass. I still don't know to this day whether that little incident affected his chances but if it did I should think that the man concerned is as embarrassed as the rest of his colleagues must be when they see just how amazingly successful Mick has been since and what a mess Dermot Browne has made of his chance by comparison."

As for Cunningham-Brown, he confesses: "When Mick first approached me I was a bit dubious. I thought 'spoilt footballer who has been used to having everything done for him by his clubs'. But I couldn't have been more wrong. He was just the opposite. He was first one in here every morning and last one out at night. He was a genuine workaholic.

"During our very first week together, I could tell there was going to be no limit as to what he could achieve. He was a good learner and a good listener – although he didn't suffer fools. More importantly, he was extremely observant and, for such an extrovert character, he had a surprisingly keen eye for detail."

That knack of being observant is the key to successful training. Horses might look the same to most people but as a trainer you soon realise that they all have distinct personalities of their own. Obviously they can't talk to you but their body language can tell you all you want to know if you learn to read it properly.

"Some people can take forever to read the signs and still not get a handle on it. Maybe Mick has that knack instinctively. He probably understands thoroughbred athletes more than most because he has been one himself."

Cunningham-Brown's comments on this subject certainly back up an enlightening passage in that marvellous book about American wonder horse Seabiscuit where its author, Laura Hillenbrand, writes: "Those unfamiliar with horses might scoff at the notion of equine pride as a silly anthropomorphism but the behaviour is unmistakable. Those who live among racehorses see it every day. Horses who lose their riders during races almost always try to win anyway, charging to the lead and sometimes bucking with pleasure as they pass their opponents. Weaning herds stampede around their paddocks several times a day, running all-out to beat one another. Even old stallions, decades away from the track, still duel with one another up and down the fences of breeding farms. And, at the races, winners prick their ears and swagger while losers show clear signs of dejection and frustration and, sometimes, even shame."

And Cunningham-Brown adds, significantly: "To be a successful trainer, you have to learn how to train owners as well as horses. And Mick has the natural social skills to do that part of the job to perfection. A lot of people probably think that the racing establishment looks down its nose at Mick Channon because he's an old footballer but I think it's the very reverse. In these days of celebrity worship it doesn't harm Mick's persona one bit that he was a big star in his playing days and, later, on television. Owners like that kind of aura to rub off on them too. I mean, even Her Majesty the Queen must be a fan of his, too, after selling him her stable.

"Another of Mick's strengths is that he is brave and is ready to take a chance on placing his runners. If you wait for the right going, the right distance, the right opposition, the right grade and the right draw on the right track you can finish up waiting for ever. But Mick will often take the plunge and find out the hard way with startlingly successful results. There is an old saying in this game that training horses consists of hours of misery and moments of magic. Well, I certainly experienced some magic moments when Mick was here with me."

CHAPTER TWENTY-FIVE
EARLY OWNERS

Mick Channon's magic moment finally came in the autumn of 1989 when, after applying for a trainer's licence again – this time successfully – he found a stable in Lambourn, Berkshire, which is situated in what has become known as "the valley of the racehorse". And if ever that renowned bravery of his was to be put to the test it was now. Britain was still in recovery from one of its worst-ever economic recessions and impoverished racehorse trainers were dropping like flies in the plague of bankruptcies that was bedevilling the country.

On the plus side, if you were a risk taker like Channon you could pick up the odd bargain. And in his typical, do-or-die style, within three years he had ensconced himself in not just one but three different stables. Those magic moments to which Ken Cunningham-Brown had referred were centred mainly on the steady flow of winners he and Mick turned out between them in their time together. And as a dozen of those stable inhabitants were a motley mix of Flat racers and jumpers either owned by

Mick or syndicates he had formed, he obviously took them with him when he moved on.

Whilst with Cunningham-Brown, Mick had moved into a house in Stockbridge and virtually on to Cunningham-Brown's doorstep. He reckoned that if he was going to have to drive Ken's horsebox to tracks all over the country, as he had done for the Bakers, then he might as well cut down the rest of his travelling as much as he could. This time, he took his current wife, Jill, with him as a live-in partner. Jill and Mick had married in 1992, with Mick's son, Michael, being chosen to be best man at the wedding.

The first little stable Mick unearthed for himself could only be described as a jewel in terms of history, prestige and tradition in that it belonged to that iconic old jumps trainer Fulke Walwyn and was at a celebrated site called Saxon Gate. The only drawback for Mick, however, was that the vacant 25 boxes that he was leasing were in the vacant bottom yard and were far from glistening.

They were, in fact, so run-down and dilapidated that he nearly had to abandon them before he had even got started. No sooner had he taken over there than a freak hurricane blew the roof tiles all over the stable like so much shrapnel from an exploded shell. And Mick had to instruct his skeleton staff of stable lads to wear their skullcaps at all times for their own safety. Most of the roof blew off with the result that Mick and the lads had to turn themselves into emergency roofing tilers before the place was habitable for either man or beast. To say he started from scratch was to understate his plight. His "office" was a builder's portacabin and with no office staff he had to do his own entries for races in which he intended to run his horses. And he needed them to start winning post-haste so that he could fill the dozen empty boxes. He began touting for business by bullying friends and neighbours to buy into the 1990 season as owners.

Back in the days when Mick had lived at Jamesmead, Barry Taylor's garden backed on to his and as this pair had been the joint owners of Super Zoom, that fabulous 33 to 1 winner at Chepstow, Barry was an obvious target. Taylor, a close friend of Alan Ball and his wife Lesley, happened to be managing director of a leading photographic company so Super Zoom was aptly named. As this had been his first-ever venture into the racing game, Barry was, predictably, one of the first on Mick's hit list of potential clients when Mick started up on his own. And for good measure he began introducing other prospective owners to Mick. One of these was society photographer Koo Stark, the one-time girlfriend of Prince Andrew, who bought a horse that she also appropriately named Slow Exposure.

But this one soon belied its name by winning a very good maiden in that first season. And as Miss Stark was sponsored by Mr Taylor's company, he again had good reason to be grateful for Mick's training skills. So much so that the moment Super Zoom's half sister, Rohita, came under the hammer he bought her too and she became the first Channon horse to get into the frame in a prestigious Listed race a couple of years later. But soaraway Channon had already got off to a rocket-fired start to his new life by notching up an across-the-card double in the very first month of that new 1990 Flat season. They were with Golden Scissors and Wessex Warrior, who both won over two miles at Beverley and Wincanton respectively. Golden Scissors was ridden by John Reid and Paul Holley piloted the Warrior in a National Hunt "bumper" flat race.

Golden Scissors was owned jointly by Kevin Keegan and his close personal friend Trevor Mitchell. Mitchell, incidentally, is the Southampton-based hairdresser who – according to your taste in coiffeur – was famous or infamous for the bubble perms sported by Saints' England internationals Keegan, Peter Shilton and

Charlie George. And he also takes responsibility for those long flowing locks favoured by our hero, Channon himself, in the 1970s, that decade of flared trousers, kipper ties and other generally way-out men's fashions. Mr Mitchell, who already had horses with Ken Cunningham-Brown, came to his half share of Golden Scissors in a roundabout way via a winning yankee bet that he shared with Keegan one day at Salisbury races.

He explains: "My half of that win was £700 so Kevin said that if I put that back in the kitty I could have a half share with him in a horse called Fair Charter, which was then trained by Mick's old chum, David Elsworth. Fair Charter won a seller at Exeter but somebody went and bought it in the auction afterwards and I was choked. Kevin said: 'Don't worry. You can put the proceeds of the sale into a half share in a very useful two-year-old that I bred who is in Luca Cumani's yard at the moment.'

"Well, we went to Newmarket to watch this horse being ridden out and as soon as Kevin saw the work rider in action, he said: 'That kid's going to be a great rider one day', which wasn't a bad shout when you consider that the lad concerned was none other than a then 15-year-old Frankie Dettori. We duly bought the horse and, as she was going to run in my colours, we named her Golden Scissors and then switched her to Mick's new yard.

"And blow me down if Scissors didn't go and follow up that first Flat win by providing him with his first winner over the sticks, too, when Lorna Vincent rode her to victory in a novices' hurdle at Hereford later that same year. She turned out to be a money-spinner for us as a broodmare as well when we later had great fun with one of her progeny, Scissor Ridge, who also won some nice races for us." Then, to fill the Channon cup to overflowing, that Mick Quinn horse Land Sun went on to become his first two-year-old winner of that momentous inaugural season.

But Trevor claims the biggest sporting thrill that he experienced involving Mick Channon was when he played against him in a competitive match when Mick was still a teenager. "I was man-marking him and – apart from the fact that Mick scored no less than seven goals against us – I played a blinder," he laughs. As for Mick, he was soon proving that he was almost as good at registering winners as he was at scoring goals. He trained 16 horses to victory on the Flat and had six National Hunt winners as well in that first season.

Naturally, the more success he had, the more owners he attracted and he soon needed extra boxes to accommodate his newer charges. He achieved this by acquiring a second neighbouring yard called Cedar Lodge and ran the two stables in conjunction. At Cedar Lodge he found himself adjacent to Jenny Pitman's stable. She, incidentally, remembers him with affection but says he swore more often than a sailor.

Barry Taylor is quick to point out that Channon's successes were strictly the result of hard work and no little skill on his part. He explains: "Mick's great achievement was that he maximised the ability of every horse he trained. Plenty of trainers had higher-quality horses than his in their yards, but did not develop their potential. I would say that he worked harder than anybody else in the business. Obviously, as a footballer Mick had trained himself almost every day of his life and he seemed to know the process to get an equine athlete's body into the right condition especially at the beginning of each season.

"Of course, he had his critics inside the sport when he first started out. Some people thought that only inheritors, ex-guardsmen and ex-jockeys could be trainers, but no one could be more pleased than myself or any one of Mick's other owners that he has so spectacularly proved them wrong." He proved them so wrong, in fact, that the next year, 1991, he trained 22 more Flat winners and eight under National Hunt rules. And this was the year he had his first really big winner when Affair Of State won the Tattersalls Breeders Stakes in Ireland for first prize money of 500,000 Irish punts. The following year, 1992, yielded 27 Flat winners and six over the sticks.

In 1993 he trained 41 Flat winners and six more over the jumps. And by this time, because he needed to expand even more, he vacated Cedar Lodge and rented a much larger stable called Kingsdown in Upper Lambourn from which ex-ace jump jockey Jamie Osborne is now sending out his fair share of winners as resident trainer. But Mick retained his hold on Saxon Gate, where he had now become owner instead of just tenant, and he continued operating from the two different yards.

Then, after Mick and Jill's first child, Jack, was born they built their own dream house at Saxon Gate, where their daughter India was born, and which Jill so lovingly designed before her old man carted her off, virtually kicking and screaming, to West Ilsley seven years later. Others of those early owners were Peter Taplin, another shooting companion of Mick's, and Patrick Trant, a Southampton supporter who now has a horse with Mick called Le Tiss, after that more recent Saints legend Matthew Le Tissier. Incidentally, Le Tiss won at their local track, Salisbury, last September at a generous 14 to 1. Channon could not resist having a pop at Matt, though, by telling him: "I'm amazed at that nag winning – until now, I thought he was slower than you!"

Yet another of Mick's early birds was property developer John Livock, who was Kevin Keegan's doubles partner at tennis when they were neighbours in Spain some years ago. Mr Livock boasts: "I was the big server and Kevin was the retriever and we were pretty well unbeatable in that part of the world." His two current big equine hopes at West Ilsley are a colt, Top Seed, and a filly, Foot Fault. Top Seed, who has already been placed in

Listed races, is, he reports, being aimed at a lot of top races this coming season.

Another of Mr Livock's modest claims to fame is that he used to give Keegan a running commentary on his horses over his mobile telephone whenever Kevin couldn't catch the races concerned. "I even phoned him once with a commentary as he was on his way up the stairs of an aeroplane," says John. "That's how keen Kevin is on his horses." He could have said that, too, about Kevin's wife, Jean, who is an established breeder and runs horses with Channon in her own colours.

CHAPTER TWENTY-SIX

TREBLE CHANCERS

Ask any of Mick Channon's friends what his most consistent characteristic is and they will tell you it is his loyalty. Some will say he swears too much and too often, some will say he is too quick-tempered, others will rave about his generosity. But whatever his quirks – good or bad – the one truly constant virtue in his nature, they will tell you, is his loyalty. So no matter how much success he was destined to earn in his new life as a trainer, his stable doors were always going to be open to Alan Ball and Kevin Keegan, his ears were always going to be pinned back for any words of wisdom that David Elsworth and Richard Hannon might still have to offer and he was always going to be a soft touch for the hard-luck stories he might hear from any of his old "Ale House" muckers.

As for the serious mutual interest in horses that Mick, Alan and Kevin shared, it was always Bally's proud boast that he was the first of the trio past the post when it came to leading in the first winner as an owner. At the time of Mick's venture into training, he might already have had "a leg or more" of several winners and he might have jointly-owned multiple winner Man On The Run with Keegan, but when Bally proudly led three-year-old maiden Go Go Gunner into the winner's enclosure in the early 1970s he was, he believes, the first-ever professional footballer to have a horse running in his own colours. Those colours were, of course, the red and white of Arsenal, for whom Ball was then playing and Go Go Gunner, which won by four lengths at 13 to 8 favourite, gave Alan even more reason to puff out his chest because his jockey was none other than the peerless Lester Piggott.

Alan remembers: "I had previously owned a horse called Daxel when I was with Everton in the late 1960s. This was trained by Barry Hills and my co-owner was that old Evertonian, Alex Young, who was known throughout the game as the 'golden boy'. Another even more 'golden boy' I co-owned a horse with was George Best. This one was called Slim Gipsy and was trained by Ian Walker at Newmarket. But both those animals turned out to be useless.

"I later had Spill The Beans and Mornin Reserves. And I made a right balls-up of it with him by selling too early because he turned into a right good horse. So I had to wait half a lifetime to get another one better than Go Go Gunner and that came after I had been sacked from the Portsmouth manager's job not once, but twice." Here, Alan is referring to Pic Up Sticks, one of the unluckiest horses this mug punter of an author has ever done his money on. In the 2002 season this speedster finished second twice in the most unfortunate circumstances: once when a fault in the starting gates resulted in the winner's stall opening split seconds before his; and another when he was drawn on the wrong side of the course, which prevented him winning by a distance.

Ball and his business partner, William Harrison-Allan, leased Pic Up Sticks to the veterans of England's winning World Cup team, who had formed "The Club of 66" and they ran it in England's colours. They must have thought they had used up all the good luck that was ever going to come their way when that Swiss referee and his linesman from the Soviet Union ruled that Geoff Hurst's controversial shot had crossed the line against West Germany in the final all those years ago. But the horse has reverted back to Ball and Harrison-Allan's ownership and both Bally and trainer Mick are confident of a very good 2004 season with him. Ball says: "When he won at Beverley early last season, I thought: 'Here we go – this one is a proper horse – but he later broke his nose, which didn't help. He's recovered now, though, and I think he'll win some good races for us this year." But win or lose, Alan will still be very proud of him. "Pic Up Sticks ran for two seasons in England's colours and he won enough prize money to more than pay his way – and that is the most you can hope for in this game.

"I didn't go into racing like the sheikhs; it's a business to them. For me, it's sheer pleasure – the agony and the ecstasy, if you like. When a horse I own crosses the line in front, I feel as proud as if I'd just scored a winning goal for England. But when it loses, my mates who've backed it all start moaning. Mind you, Mick and Kevin and me have had a lifetime of that – celebrating in victory and keeping our heads down in defeat."

They experienced defeat in their football careers less often than most, of course, but the worst gambling disaster our intrepid trio ever suffered collectively came at a racetrack in the USA, when Channon and Channon alone was responsible for snatching defeat out of the jaws of victory. They were on a close-season tour of that country with Southampton and, on their first day off, the three of them pooled their spending money and set off for the nearest track full of punters' customary unrealistic expectations. It did not help that they had not got a clue about the local form so it was not surprising that they had lost most of the "pot" after the first three races. In desperation, they settled on a big outsider in the next to get them out of trouble.

Kevin Keegan takes up the commentary from there: "We almost rode the horse ourselves as we cheered it past the post in front and out came the credit cards as we switched drinks from beer to champagne in celebration while old clever clogs Channon went off to collect our winnings. You can imagine what Bally and I called him when he came back with a stupid look on his face and confessed that he had made a mistake at the Tote window when he put the bet on by stating the wrong number for our selection. We were so skint on the return trip that I had to dash into the hotel to borrow the taxi fare off one of the other players."

That little mishap did nothing to knock Kevin's confidence in his pal as a trainer, however. He went on record a few years later as saying: "If the champion trainer offered to train my horses for free, I would still send them to Mick Channon." Yet, ironically, Keegan was to go on to enjoy his biggest racing victory with a horse that had just switched stables from down south with Mick to up north with Mick's good mate, Dandy Nicholls. This was Funfair Wane, and it stormed home in the Tote Ayr Gold Cup at 16 to 1, netting £65,000 in prize money for the owners and breeders: Kevin and his wife Jean.

Channon explains what caused the fateful move this way: "As a two-year-old, Funfair Wane had plenty of ability – he won a decent maiden at York and then followed up in the Listed Washington Singer Stakes at Newbury. He was never an unkind horse but he was uncooperative in the sense that he was always a bit fizzy and needed to calm down. You could put your kids on him in his box but when it came to the action he often got too headstrong. Animals like this sometimes benefit from a change of scenery so I advised Kevin and Jean that they were better off taking the horse away from me and putting him with Dandy Nicholls in North Yorkshire. Dandy, as everyone in racing knows, is a wizard with sprinters and he certainly proved it again with Funfair.

"I tried to thwart him by throwing in no fewer than four of mine against him. They were Royal Millennium, Budelli, Kulachi and Pic Up Sticks, but Dandy matched me with four runners of his own and then trumped me and the rest of racing when Funfair made it a hat-trick of wins in successive years for Dandy in this daunting sprint handicap." Afterwards, Nicholls said of this star three-year-old: "I think Mick's feeling was that he would be better suited away from a big training centre like his. He's hyperactive and he was getting geed up before this race so I kept him out of the parade ring as long as I dared. If the big training regime is in his face every day, he just can't handle it. But he has a super engine and he'll be an even better horse next year."

So Funfair Wane looks like becoming a "big one" that got away from Mick. Never prone to crying over spilt milk, he simply says: "There have been others and there will be more."

CHAPTER TWENTY-SEVEN

YARD

When two-year-old filly Mail The Desert won the Group One Moyglare Stud Stakes at The Curragh in Ireland on Sunday 1 September 2002, Mick Channon's young secretary Susan Harding found herself ad-libbing a commentary from her TV set to the horse's owner, property developer John Livock, who happened to be in France at the time. Softly-spoken Irish lass Susan became so excited when her stable's horse got involved in a blanket finish that she momentarily forgot to speak at all – until the horses crossed the line and then she could only scream: "Fuck me! She's won!"

Susan will blush all the way down to her toenails when she reads this anecdote, which is related by Mr Livock himself, who says. "I was gutted to miss being at The Curragh for the sporting thrill of my lifetime but I had to turn up for a pre-arranged golf match in France. I was just lining up a birdie putt when Susan came on to my mobile to read the race for me. Needless to say, I missed the putt and was so excited myself that I had to tell someone so I immediately rang my great friend Ted Dexter on his mobile. When he answered my call, Ted let out a similar expletive to Susan but he wound up calling me all the names he could lay his tongue on because he happened to be standing on the steps at Lords Cricket Ground at the time delivering his farewell speech as President of the MCC."

Susan rarely swears but as she works all hours and has to put up with language that could blister paint off the woodwork most of the time, it is no wonder that the odd four-letter word escapes from her lips occasionally. And in this case it was entirely appropriate, as Mr Livock explains when he relates how the horse got her name. "Mick and I thought she was something special when he bought her for me. She was by a stallion called Desert Prince; her dam was Mail Boat. I dithered for ages over choosing a name for her until Mick ran out of patience with me and said: 'It's obvious, innit? Just call her Mail The Fucking Desert!' As for Ted Dexter – he is more into trotting and greyhound racing than he is horses – but he was with me at Windsor when she won her maiden and he had £100 to win at 7 to 2 so naturally he followed up on her after that."

Telephonically, Susan is Channon's first line of defence at West Ilsley. It is she who has to deal with owners, fodder purveyors and the like. And, of course, jockeys who want to get on the stables' pride and joy whenever they can. In addition to her administrative skills, Susan is a useful work rider, too, and has partnered most of the stable stars on the gallops. The daughter of Irish point-to-point trainer John Joe Harding and one of a family of eight children, she cut her milk teeth in County Cork, riding a chestnut pony called Lucky with the Avondhu and Duhallow hunts.

In those days, she never imagined herself working in an office. "I just wanted to be with horses full stop," she says. "I had to be dragged by the ear by my parents to the secretarial college at Mallow." After two years at the Rathbarry Stud, Susan moved to England, arriving at Ian Williams' stable and on to Robert Cowell's Newmarket base. Realising that if her star was to shine she had to join a larger stable, she wrote to the top 20 trainers in England. Most of them replied but Channon was the only one to phone her and invite her down to West Ilsley. Now she lives there and has to be ready every morning at 5.45am to ride out with the "first lot", which heads for the Berkshire Downs at 7.30am.

She says of her life with Mick: "He is different in the way he does things with the two-year-olds. It's like being out hunting, going up the gallops in January, with the boss sorting them out from an early stage." Later, she deals mainly with making entries for the stable's runners. "This can be really manic," she says, "because of the large number of horses we have here – entering them at home and abroad." If she fails to get through to Weatherbys – the Jockey Club agents – by the required deadline, a horse does not run. And that is the ultimate nightmare for a racing secretary, who then has to face her irate employer. "Luckily, I've never had a cross word with Mick yet. If he has a go at you – that's it. If you stay quiet, it's all forgotten within five minutes," she says gratefully.

Another young, Irish horse lover who has good reason to be grateful to Channon is rookie trainer Mark Wallace, who has just completed his first season with the sensational tally of more than 20 winners to his name. Wallace was Mick's assistant for nearly six years before branching out on his own with just 12 horses and overdraft worries to his name. But already he has increased his string to 35 and has attracted owners of the calibre of Sheikh Rashid, the eldest son of Sheikh Mohammed, John Magnier, Michael Tabor and Charles St George to his roster.

A doctor's son from Tipperary, 30-year-old Wallace now rents

Newmarket's Woodland Stables from retired trainer Di Haine, but he readily admits; "I would never have been able to start training at all without Mick's help. He has sent me horses and recommended me to some of his owners. Mick is a proper person. If you worked hard and he knew you were on his side he was just grand. But if you told Mick lies, you didn't survive. He gave me the confidence to start up on my own. But financially it was a nightmare.

"You have to do deals with new owners, charging half training fees. I bought those dozen horses on spec and had sleepless nights for three months. Getting them sold again was the frightening thing. Some people in Newmarket thought I was mad but I had my yearlings cantering in October. That's what Mick and Aidan O'Brien do so I've just copied off the best. I hate getting beaten in races and that's the main thing that rubbed off on me from Mick. I always try to book the best jockeys and Kieren Fallon has ridden half a dozen winners for me."

Another Irishman, Paul Deegan, has replaced Wallace as Mick's assistant trainer. Still in his early twenties, Paul has been "thrown in at the deep end" but has several head lads to help him out and as many as 40 gallops riders at the height of the season, of whom at least 30 live in either a house or a flat on Mick's property.

Overseeing them all is 44-year-old attractive blonde Mrs Gill Hedley, who is Mick's "right-hand lady" but has an official title of financial director of their bloodstock company. She says: "West Ilsley is quite simply my life. I put in 12 hours a day here and love every minute of it." It so happens that her husband, who travels a lot in his work in the electronics business, has an allergy to horses that brings him out in a rash so he seldom goes anywhere near the stables to interrupt Gill in her work.

A qualified accountant, Gill commuted for eight years from Winchester to London to work in an office there but as she has always been "animal crackers" and badly needed a change of scenery, she applied for a book-keeping vacancy with Mick and got it. That was nearly ten years ago and she says now: "I can't believe how far we've come since then. It's all quite unbelievable, really. As our success has snowballed we sometime get a wee bit nervous that we have created a monster. But Mick is so upbeat that that scary mood never lasts long.

"I don't want to sound as if I'm grovelling," she says, "but Mick is the most inspirational person I've ever worked for. Working with him is brilliant; he's always setting targets and once we've reached one it's on to the next. We never get complacent here and start thinking that we are top of the heap. His enthusiasm is contagious and it spreads right through the stable — sometimes you think even the horses can feel it.

"And it's particularly rewarding for me because I deal with most of the things he doesn't want to be bothered with. That is not to belittle his business acumen, though. I mean, he is very switched-on himself in that area. He comes up with the vision and goals and I look after the detail. A big part of my work here can be called public relations but although I like people well enough, I am absolutely potty about horses — that's why I'm in seventh heaven here. When people say that racing is more than a job, that it is a way of life, they are right. And it is perhaps even more enthralling for me because I wasn't born into the racing game like the majority of people who work in it were.

"And as for the horses themselves, well, non-racing people will find this hard to believe but I swear to you that every one of our almost 150 horses here has a different personality. So, just like people, you are bound to like some more than others. And my personal pin-up boy is Najeebon, whose stable door is bang opposite my office window so I see him every day. He's big and handsome, has a cheeky personality and a kind face and I love him to bits. And what's more, I don't feel guilty that he's my favourite. After all, racing is all about favourites and also-rans isn't it?"

The same could be said about all the stable lads and lasses and work riders who populate Gill's working day, but she is understandably staying mum when it comes to picking out favourites from this lot of mostly hyperactive youngsters. I say hyperactive because one thing that Mick will not tolerate around him are "lazy sods" of either sex. "Stubborn is OK," he says, "In fact, I've never met a good sportsman or sportswoman who didn't have a stubborn streak. It goes with the territory. As for their behaviour, well as rowdy as they can be at times, when it comes to booze, me and my old Ale House muckers have spilt more down our ties than that mob here have ever drunk.

"When that lot I told you about got pissed and fell in the duck pond us Ale House lads would have only just been getting into our stride at that stage of the game. In this day and age, though, it is the recreational drugs I have to watch out for. I mean, it's part of the culture now, innit? If I came across any hard-drug takers, they'd obviously have to go. But most of today's kids seem to smoke the odd roll-up of wacky baccy. I won't let them do it around here, though, I don't allow smoking of any kind in any part of this yard for the obvious safety reasons.

"I like to see them reasonably smartly dressed too. I don't want to see any scruffy so-and-sos cluttering up the place. That must be a hangover from my days under Lawrie McMenemy." But when I remind him of the T-shirt stunt he pulled against Lawrie with Alan Ball and Kevin Keegan on that American tour all those years ago his only defence is a guilty smile at his own grumpy-old-man style of hypocrisy.

An issue that makes him feel older than ever, though, he confesses, is the recent rumpus over Rio Ferdinand's missed drug test. This took Mick back to the time when, during his second spell as a Southampton player, he was one of the first professional footballers ever to be subjected to a routine drug test. And to say things were different back then is to understate matters. "I simply saw red and refused to take it at first," recalls Mick. "Back then it was still regarded as an insult by most of us to our standing as people and players to have to suffer this sort of stigma. And that's the way I took it. God, I'd been playing the game long enough without deserving to be suspected of being some kind of a pillhead.

"Taking real drugs was against everything I've ever stood for or believed in. It causes so much pain and heartache to so many kids that the thought of it still appals me. Mind you," he adds, "everyone seemed to regard this testing business so casually back then that I'll always remember the bloke from the FA saying: 'Well, don't worry, you can always get someone else to pee in the bottle for you.'

"I then started to see the black humour in the situation and joked: 'In that case, I'd better do it myself just in case any of my mates really are on something dodgy.' But seriously, I still don't see how you could take the drugs that are a blight on the lives of young people today and still be a top footballer. I know about steroids and unscrupulous athletes taking them – but throwing the shot or the javelin wouldn't have been much use to me. I don't believe that drug abuse can possibly be widespread in football – after all, taking them would be more of a hindrance than a help to a footballer. Even the fastest players weren't interested in breaking the world sprint record, either.

"Mind you, there had already been one hell of a stink over some alleged drug taking by that Scottish wing wizard, Willie Johnston, during the 1978 World Cup finals in Argentina. Poor little Willie had been kicked out of the tournament and packed off home for taking a so-called illegal drug. Well, two City men were in that same Scottish squad as Johnston. They were my best Maine Road pal, Asa Hartford, and our cultured defender, Willie Donachie.

"I'm sure Willie Johnston didn't think twice when he took the tablets that got him so publicly shown-up like that. But there was absolute panic in the City dressing room when he was exposed because the majority of our players had been advised to take this same substance – whatever it was – for ages without anyone ever dreaming of telling us it was illegal.

"Anyway, when Willie's predicament hit the headlines, the club physios couldn't open the medicine cupboards quickly enough to throw away everything that even resembled a tablet that could get us into trouble if and when drug testing was suddenly brought in, which it eventually was, of course. But I can assure the FA or anyone else who is interested that it wasn't even a soft drug we were taking let alone a so-called hard one. And somehow I don't think that today's players, knowing all the sophisticated advances that have been made on drug detection, would be any more inclined to put their careers in jeopardy than we were – even less so, I should think, when you consider the monster salaries they would be endangering."

At this juncture, a memory flits into Mick's mind that causes his expression to change instantly from a frown into a grin. And he says, almost apologetically: "I know this is a serious discussion but every time I talk about drugs, I can't resist remembering one of the funniest, sick, racing jokes I ever heard. It is set in the time when doping was rife back in the 1960s. This trainer has got a certainty going in the 2.30 and has told his aristocratic owner to have the Duchess's tiara on it. But when the illustrious owner comes down to the parade ring to watch the jockey mount, he sees the trainer sliding something into the horse's mouth.

"He is beside himself with rage at the sight of this and berates the trainer, calling him a blackguard and worse. But the trainer says: 'Look, your grace, it's only a lump of sugar I've given to the nag. He does his best work on it. It's totally harmless – taste it yourself.' And with that he puts another lump to the owner's lips. Then after taking a lick of yet another lump himself, he says: 'You just relax, your grace. Stick your arse on your shooting stick, watch the race and then go and collect.' Then, with the owner suitably placated, he lifts the jockey aboard and blows in his ear, whispering: 'Keep him on a tight rein until the last furlong, son, and then give him his head. And remember, should anything pass you it could only possibly be me or the Duke of Fucking Norfolk!'"

CHAPTER TWENTY-EIGHT

LOGIC

For all Mick Channon's macho protestations about the prospect of permitting himself to go weak at the knees or sloppily starry-eyed over any member of the equine species, he finds it impossible to deny that he came perilously close to losing his heart to one young filly. Her name was Queen's Logic. Bred in the purple, she was so fast and so fit that every time he entered her in a race she was – to use that graphic description favoured by so many American horseplayers – ready to run a hole in the wind.

That "Logic" part of her name could not have been more appropriate. For, according to every form expert in the country, she had only to face the starter to become Mick's first Classic winner. Having run unbeaten four times in the very highest class as a two-year-old and then won just as convincingly in her first "prep" race as a three-year-old, she was primed to land the 1000 Guineas at Newmarket in May 2002, pulling the proverbial cart.

Sadly, however, instead of facing the starter, Queen's Logic found herself facing the vet on the morning of her date with destiny, as the victim of a foot injury that she sustained by stepping on a stone in the stable yard. This freak accident turned out to be the first in a series of mishaps that summer which culminated in a cough serious enough to force her retirement as early as July. So she had to be led off to stud without so much as having fluttered her eyelashes at the racing immortality that had once seemed her birthright.

A Classic winner is, for Channon, the racing trainer, the equivalent of not just an England cap but League-and-Cup-winner's double medals for Channon the footballer. It is racing's holy grail. And it still eludes him. The stricken filly's owner, Jaber Abdullah, was quick to attempt to tear the blinkers off the claustrophobic little world of racing and put Queen's Logic's misfortune into perspective by saying: "Aeroplanes fall out of the sky and people get killed." But that over-dramatic choice of metaphor only succeeded in upping the ante in some racing circles, most particularly with some of the more hard-nosed punters who were left holding worthless ante-post vouchers in her name.

Channon consoled himself with a "'tis better to have loved and lost"-style lover's lament by saying: "I would rather have had this wonderful filly for five races than not at all. She retires as an unbeaten Group One winner and there aren't many horses you can say that about. She is certain to be in demand as a broodmare and I look forward to training her offspring one day." Then, with typical optimism, he added: "Meanwhile, there's always next year." And little did he know it then, but 12 months later he was to come even closer to that tantalising first Classic triumph.

One outstanding success he was able to enjoy in 2002, however, was to run up his first century of domestic winners in a single Flat season. And that was a feat that even Dick Hern, who died in May of that year, was never able to achieve for the illustrious West Ilsley stable. That 100th winner came at Yarmouth on September 17 when Najeebon, Gill Hedley's favourite horse, won a six-furlong maiden at 14 to 1.

Channon found himself watching that little moment of history in the prosaic surroundings of a betting shop. He explains: "I had runners at my local track, Salisbury, and as I fancied them more than Najeebon I gave Yarmouth a miss. I found myself waiting for the photo-finish involving one of mine when I suddenly remembered that Najeebon's race was due off. So I took myself off to the television in the course betting-shop as fast as my arthritic feet could carry me and arrived just in time to see him storming home in front. And because he was an outsider it was as quiet as a cathedral in there as he crossed the line – except for me, that is. I was roaring my head off, of course."

That momentous victory took Mick's mind back to the time when he notched his 100th goal. That was at Goodison Park in an end-of-season 3–0 win for Southampton against Everton. He recalls: "Unfortunately, that win didn't stop us from getting relegated. And we went down that year with Manchester United, of all people."

But whether they came yesterday or half a lifetime ago, Channon is never one to dwell on disappointments. That is why when he gets round to reviewing the 2002 season from a safer distance in time, he is now able, in retrospect, to write off the whole Queen's Logic saga as "no more than a massive kick in the goolies for me. It was much worse for the owner, of course, in that, if she had been a stallion, she would potentially have been almost literally worth her weight in gold whereas now he can only have one foal per year from her. Still, I suppose that's as pointless as saying that if your aunt had had bollocks, she'd have been your uncle," he grins.

"I prefer to look back on the party we had at West Ilsley when we notched up that century. It was free drinks for everyone in the stable in our local pub that night and sore heads for everyone the next morning, of course. There were no more sore feelings, though. How could there be when nearly every week we had three or four winners or more and some weeks a winner a day. We had that Group One winner, Mail The Desert, and some Group Two winners too. And then we had winning individuals Budelli and Joint Statement who both ran up a sequence of successes."

But the time for reflection is strictly rationed in racing. Jockeys have to have the metaphorical equivalent of an alarm clock wedged into their brains to send them scurrying off like little clockwork men to get mounted again every half hour. And then they have to have their foot glued to the accelerator of their cars as they dash from day to evening meetings. For betting shop punters it's even worse, of course. They barely have time to draw breath between races and for many Flat trainers nowadays no sooner do some of their charges stop running on turf than they are racing again on the all-weather tracks.

And unlike the soccer close-season when, back in his less hectic playing days, he could swan around for most of the summer, there is barely time for Mick, his wife Jill and their two children to squeeze in a holiday before he is back out there treading the grass again – breaking in yearlings and putting the newest crop of two-year-olds through their paces.

"And for me, this is by far the most fascinating period of any year," says Mick. "I feel the years roll off me as I sense the young ones' emotions. Once they have been broken in you just know that they are dying to do the business for you. If only we could talk to each other, I know what they would be telling me. They would be saying: 'Now that I've got a saddle on my back, I know that this is what I was born for.' And I would tell them: 'I know, too, because that's the way I felt when I first kicked a football around.' "

Then he adds: "They are my fame academy, there are potential David Beckhams and Denise Lewises among them just waiting to be discovered. And, on a good day, this makes me feel as proud as the youth team coach at Manchester United must feel. But I must confess that on bad days, when the old arthritis is really playing me up, my mind wanders back to my own 'old arse' days when in pre-season training runs all the kids would be leading the pack, keen as mustard, while us 'old arses' would mutter to each other: 'Don't worry, in a few months time they'll be wise enough to settle in at the back with us.' But we knew in our hearts that we'd have spent a fortune to get back that natural zest they possessed. Now, though, even at the crack of dawn on the greyest of days, the good vibrations the two-year-olds throw off with their bucking and kicking for joy are always contagious enough to give me the necessary buzz to cope with another day."

CHAPTER TWENTY-NINE
JOCKEYS

Leave out the obvious choices, such as living legends Kieren Fallon and Frankie Dettori, and then ask any punter in any betting shop who is his favourite present-day jockey and it's odds-on he'll pick the one who rode the last winner for him. For the whole concept of what makes good, bad and indifferent riders is that subjective. Almost everyone seems to have a different opinion. Even leading trainers like Mick Channon have difficulty picking their favourites. He admits to being very flexible on the subject of which jockeys ride which horses for him. The main considerations are the cross-section of owners he needs to keep happy and the large number of horses in his care. And for those reasons he prefers not to have a stable jockey attached to the yard.

Sometimes the choices he makes can cause bad feeling and temperamental outbursts from some of the jocks. But Channon simply shrugs his shoulders and says: "They wouldn't be human if they didn't complain, would they? In my old job, us players threw our toys out of our prams on a regular basis if we were dropped from the first team. And as for the poor old horses, they just don't have a say in the matter, do they?"

The most publicised row Channon is supposed to have had with any jockey was with the young Australian Craig Williams a couple of seasons ago. Williams came to this country as a virtual unknown and was quickly turned into star material under Mick's patronage – until the national press reported that the pair had fallen out and that Williams had returned to Australia because of it.

Mick's version of the situation is that it was not really a row at all and simply an instance where there was no option but for he and the jockey to say goodbye. He explains it this way: "One Sunday I wanted Craig to go up north to Redcar to ride an awkward horse called Kings Signal, which he had previously won on for me. But he said he'd rather go to Kempton to ride two for James Fanshawe. So I simply replied: 'You'd better ride all of his in future then – so fuck off!' As I value loyalty above all else, I was not going to stand there arguing with him. I had given him his break over here and I thought that I wasn't asking too much of him to do me this favour.

"But it was his decision not to and I respect him for that. I always respect other people's opinions even if I happen to think they are talking bollocks. But opinions sometimes have consequences and when they do you have to live with them. Craig started saying: 'Yes, but...' But I said: 'This issue is not negotiable any more. The tail doesn't wag the dog round here.' And that was that. This didn't mean that I was going to hate Craig forever more because I had behaved the way he did myself often enough when I was younger. Looking back now, I can see what a horrible fucker I must have seemed at times – an out-and-out prima donna. I thought I was top dog and now I look back from a boss's point of view and realise just what an arsehole I must have appeared to Lawrie McMenemy and other managers at times.

"But I suppose when you look at most of human behaviour, it's simply a case of 'but for the grace of God go I, isn't it?' I mean, look at that almighty rumpus between Roy Keane and Mick McCarthy that split the Irish nation in the last World Cup. When I was a player myself I'd have been 100 per cent behind Roy but now I tend to view it through Mick's eyes."

Embarrassingly for Channon, the boot was on the other foot in a more recent riding-arrangement dispute and he found himself piggy in the middle when one of his more regular riders, Steve Drowne, was jocked off Mick's best horse, Zafeen, for the St James's Palace Stakes at Royal Ascot in 2003. It was to have been the ride of Drowne's life – one of Europe's premier mile races worth more than £150,000 to the winner and more than £10,000 for the winning jockey's percentage.

Mick's current pride and joy had already carried Drowne to success in Newbury's prestigious Mill Reef Stakes the previous season and, as recorded earlier here, had come within three-quarters-of-a-length of winning last year's 2000 Guineas at Newmarket on him before failing to handle gluepot conditions in the Irish Guineas. But Zafeen's owner, Jaber Abdullah, decided that his star miler needed a different rider at Ascot and instructed his trainer to that effect. And as it turned out, he was vindicated. Steve had to sit in the Ascot weighing room watching on television as his replacement, Darryll Holland, won the race.

Almost the first thing Channon did after this triumph was to find words of consolation for poor Drowne. "I feel very sorry for Steve. The only way I can console him is by still putting him on my horses in future as often as I can. I can't do anything else about this. You have to take your chance with luck in any sport. The horse's bad run in the Irish Guineas was no fault of Steve's or anyone else. I knew that run was all wrong and I was worried that there was something wrong with Zafeen. But all credit to everyone at West Ilsley for bringing him to such a peak for this race."

Understandably, Drowne's initial reaction was a little less than restrained. Having returned to the saddle after suffering a badly broken leg two seasons earlier, this win would have provided the perfect climax to that courageous comeback. The hurt of it all was there to be seen and heard when he said: "I was gutted, especially after I'd done nothing wrong on the horse. You can imagine how I felt when I had to sit and watch someone else win on him. For an hour or so, I was asking myself: 'Why do I bother with this game, why do I traipse around riding work at five o'clock every morning just to have this happen to me?' "

But later in the season, as he rode winner after winner to become one of the top half-dozen jockeys in the land, he reflected: "Losing a top ride happens to every jockey but you just have to come back stronger and for some strange reason I've been making all the right moves since then."

But it has turned out that since then, whatever moves he has made, he has made most of them without Mick's help. For although both men insist that there is absolutely no bad feeling between them, there can be little doubt that this last quip of Drowne's sounded suspiciously like the equivalent of a two-fingered salute of defiance in Channon's direction. And consequently it came as no surprise in racing circles that of all Mick's mountain of winners in the second half of the 2003 season you could have counted on your fingers the number Steve Drowne rode for him.

It could have been so different for their working relationship, of course, if the ill-fated Queen's Logic had fulfilled her potential with Drowne on her back because the idea of him losing the ride on any subsequent stars of Jaber Abdullah's would have been unthinkable.

Ted Durcan came in for the rides on the bulk of the Channon

horses late last summer and autumn and he visited the winner's enclosure on a regular basis as a result of Mick's flourishing purple patch of a finish to the season. Durcan, a champion jockey in Dubai, came under the same tutelage as the legendary Tony McCoy, at Jim Bolger's yard in Wexford. He and McCoy are still great friends and, ironically, Tony has been to see Ted more times than the other way round because the previously luckless Durcan has sustained even more injuries during his Flat racing career than his daredevil mate has done over the jumps.

Another Channon regular is the emerging young star, Chris Catlin. And, as there is nothing Mick enjoys more than geeing up his boys the way managers used to wind him up in his playing days, I sensed he was putting on a bit of a show for me when he invited me into the parade ring at Goodwood as he was giving Chris his instructions. Catlin, a quietly-spoken, well-mannered boy, had no idea who I was, of course, and it turned out that this particular horse was owned by Mick himself but Catlin had obviously temporarily forgotten that as he nervously tapped his whip against his leg and cocked an ear towards his guv'nor.

Looking deadly serious, Mick rasped: "Now if you know what's good for you, son, you'd better win on this one. The trainer might be a nice fellow but the owner here," he said, nodding towards me, "can be a right nasty bastard." Catlin managed to steer the animal concerned into a place and Mick chuckled afterwards and said: "That earned me a few grand so it was better than having the horse stuck in the stable at home. But now you're going to have to go down to the unsaddling enclosure and commiserate with the kid for the bad luck he had in not winning for you."

On another occasion, in 2003, Mick and I were at Salisbury together to see a mare he owns and trains, by the name of Fast Foil, win a race while she was in season. Imagine my surprise when a voice over the tannoy boomed: "Will Mr Peter Batt, the representative of the owner, please come up to be presented with the winning trophy?" Afterwards people I hadn't seen for years came from everywhere to congratulate me and say things like: "I thought you were dead" and other such befitting sentiments.

This happy little stunt of Mick's inevitably reminded me of a much less salubrious experience I'd had at Salisbury races many years earlier. It was when Portsmouth won promotion under Alan Ball and I arranged to meet him at the races next day to interview him about his triumph. When I arrived at the course Bally had not yet shown. This was back in the worst of my out-of-control drinking and gambling days and I could not go anywhere near the bookies because of the size of the debts I still owed to several of them. So I hid away up in the stands having a few quid on the Tote when this message came over the tannoy loud and clear: "Would Mr. Peter Batt please report to the Clerk of the Course as soon as possible?"

Without stopping to think about the consequences, I hurried down to the clerk's office only to find a couple of different bookies' men waiting to collar me for the money I owed their guv'nors. It turned out that Bally had got so pissed celebrating promotion the night before that he was still in a nightclub and had got his mate, Peter Osgood, to ring the track and ask me to meet him there instead.

For races up north, Channon usually relies on that ultra-reliable rider Tony Culhane to do the business for him. He has the utmost respect for the skill and strength of this model professional but found himself having to leap to Culhane's defence one day when the jockey uncharacteristically committed the almost unpardonable error of dropping his hands on a horse called True Courage at Pontefract for another stable.

The next morning Channon said: "I feel really sorry for Tony. A jockey has never done that to me and admittedly I might feel slightly differently if he did. But Tony is in bits today – the same as I was when I missed a penalty or two. No matter what the cynics say, no sportsman I know fucks up on purpose. Although, in racing, I do think that the practice of a jockey winning by the minimal margin possible to stop a horse going up the weights is a load of nonsense. You can't fool the handicapper and if you win by a length hard on the bridle, he will put you up what he thinks you are worth."

The practice of employing only freelances, as Channon does, is inevitably going to bring its ups and downs for the partnership both in and out of the saddle, however. And there was a big hiccup in the fledgling career of Dean Corby, an apprentice who burst into the racing headlines by riding 35 winners for his mentor, Mick, in his first season in the big time. But he left Channon early last year to move up the road to neighbouring trainer Hughie Morrison in East Ilsley. Channon took Corby's departure philosophically, saying: "Young Dean found he couldn't take the ribbing from the other lads in the yard any more. Well, that's part and parcel of this sporting life. He should have been in some of the dressing rooms I was in as a kid. Anyway, he got restless, and like so many other youngsters in any sport, he thought he could run before he could walk. Some of his friends misled him and told him he was better than Steve Drowne or even Kieren Fallon."

But after only ten winning rides from more than 180 mounts Corby headed back west to Channon looking for a second chance. Mick put him up on his old mate Budelli, on whom he had run up a succession of wins, and the pair were promptly back in the winner's enclosure together again. Mick sums all this up by saying: "I am chuffed to have him back and he will ride plenty of my horses." He then adds the ominous warning, "I've got other promising kids such as Sam Hitchcott and Brian O'Neil now, though."

When he described Hitchcott as "promising," Mick was making a massive understatement. But at the time he spoke he was not to know that this much-more-than-capable little apprentice would go on to ride his game stayer, Misternando, to no fewer than ten victories last season – the record number for any one horse during that campaign. We all know that jockeys are supposed to be tiny, but baby-faced Hitchcott is tiny and then some. At 21, he has to take his passport with him on a night out to prove that he is old enough to drink.

But he was old enough and big enough to ride more than 40 winners, earning him more than £50,000 in prize money and riding fees and enabling him to finish second to Ryan Moore in the apprentices' table. He even notched up a couple of trebles at major tracks like Goodwood and Ayr. And all this after suffering one of the most horrific-looking falls of the season when Misternando bumped into the rail at Yarmouth in July and pitched Sam over the top of it and into no-man's-land beyond the running track.

Channon has no doubt that if his latest human stable star can continue to make the most of every opportunity that comes his way and then learn to live with the travel weariness and stay the course through the wear and tear of the manic daily grind that is the modern jockey's lot he can become one of the sport's greats. Young Sam, who started his career in the smaller stable of Mick Easterby in Yorkshire, reciprocates by echoing the words of most of those who have gone before him by describing his new boss as "hard but very fair" and he will get no arguments from Channon about that.

CHAPTER THIRTY

TWO GAME FILLIES

The first thing to be said about Mick Channon as an employer is that his is very much an equal opportunities outfit. He might have spent his youth in soccer surrounded by hairy arses and jockstraps but he invited petticoat power into his life the moment he switched to the racing game. Two game fillies who have been with him since day one and beyond are Lesley White and Gill Richardson. Lesley began as babysitter for Nicky and Michael junior and Gill was the "girl Friday" in his first office.

They are now travelling head lass and chief buyer respectively. Lesley, who still lives near Mick, is his representative on all the northern tracks and drives their horsebox endless miles to prepare every runner for the day's action and then get them safely back home as well as looking after their owners in the process. Gill is Mick's eyes and ears at the yearling and two-year-old sales that are, of course, the make–or–break end of his business.

When I accompany them to the Doncaster yearling sales that

are held annually during the St Leger meeting, it is like stepping back in time. We book into the Grand St Leger Hotel that is almost as ancient as the old race itself. Some of the stables with grander pretensions stay at newer, posh watering holes but Mick prefers the genial conviviality here that rivals "the crack" at the Cheltenham hostelries during the Festival there. Talk about atmosphere! You step out of the front door, cross the road and you're on the track. You go out the back door, down a couple of steps and you are slap bang in the middle of the sales stables. Unfortunately, my room overlooks them and I am kept awake most of the night by young colts and fillies presumably crying for their mummies. They sound to me like so many nanny goats shitting on corrugated iron. But for any potential owner who might buy one of them and win a fortune with it in prize money, they will obviously look back on that nerve-racking sound as if it were coming from a heavenly choir.

And how do you come by such a creature? The first requirement is to have someone like Gill with you to mark your card, of course. But first and foremost, you must be prepared to stand your round. For these Doncaster yearling sales are as much a social event as a serious business appointment.

People pay as much as £50,000 for the best there is on offer but everyone who's anyone in the training and bloodstock agent ranks gathers there for a traditional booze-up, too, in the bar that is actually situated on the premises of the sales ring itself.

Gill is steeped in horse sense. She was raised in Yorkshire, where her parents, Austin and Betty, are well-known breeders and buyers. She now works on a freelance basis for Mick as a buyer in her own right which obviously presents her with much more responsibility than her old office job for him did. But she says: "You mustn't let the responsibility or the pressure get to you or you will soon crack up. I've made plenty of mistakes but you have to shrug them off and balance them with the really good buys. The crazy thing about this business is that you have only five minutes to make up your mind as to whether a horse is worth a second look or not.

"They are led from their boxes on request and walk only a few yards before you are expected to declare an interest or not. One of the first things my father ever told me was that if a horse can't walk properly it can't gallop either. So if they shuffle or are cross-legged or pigeon-toed, you don't give them a second look. I will look at as many as 100 horses a day during the three days here so I have to maintain total concentration."

Gill's boyfriend is the popular National Hunt jockey Andrew Thornton and believe it or not she favours horses that look like Andrew or Mick. She smiles as she explains: "Both Andrew and Mick have kind faces and that's the second thing I look for in a horse after I've watched them walking. They must have a kind face and generous eyes which tell you that they will give you everything in a race. My mother was once savaged in the unsaddling enclosure at York by one of her horses so I just don't want to know them if they have an evil eye. You want to see determination in their eyes, but definitely not meanness. A mean streak might be OK in a champion boxer, but a mean-spirited horse is usually more trouble than it's worth.

"That doesn't mean that I think some horses are out-and-out rogues, far from it. I think the mean ones are that way because of some traumatic experience they may have encountered during their early lives – just like humans, really."

But according to Channon, the traumas any of these horses may have suffered is as nothing compared to the aggravation they are about to bring to him as soon as he gets his purchases home.

He explains: "You need at least four or five months' constant work before you can turn a raw yearling into a racing machine.

They go through most of the little physical ailments that kids do. They get ringworm, snotty noses, coughs, measles, chickenpox and even acne. And, more seriously, if you ask them to do too much too soon they get sore shins like a lot of young footballers do because their immature bones can't stand the strain of too much exertion.

"First you have to take them through all the basic steps to full mobility by teaching them to walk, to trot, to canter and then to gallop. So the next time you see an animal move like poetry in motion on a racecourse just remember what agonies the poor old 'poet' had to go through to create that spectacle. In the winter, we put people on their backs and their centre of gravity moves. That's why jockeys stand up: because it makes it easier for the horse to travel as naturally as possible.

"It's an even more hit and miss process than grooming young footballers for stardom. I mean, by the time a young footballer reaches the professional level he can obviously meet the basic requirements; otherwise he would not have got that far. But with horses all we have to gamble on is breeding, looks, instinct and prayers. But it all gives me such an adrenalin rush that I wouldn't change it for the world. Come November, we switch from the daily grind of trying to churn out winners to breaking horses in and you don't get back to the normal routine until the next March.

"When a senior citizen such as Sir Bobby Robson says he is addicted to football, I think what he really means is that he is addicted to adrenaline. OK, we all need a daily routine to help us stay sane, but in this business all manner of things can happen unexpectedly. Someone might suddenly want to buy a horse from me or sell me one. Then I'll have to look at the going and decide do I run a particular horse at Ayr or Newmarket? And the next thing I could hear is that one of my horses has gone lame and while all this is going on via my mobile phone I have to be in the

Land Rover out on the gallops supervising the training. So it's not a whole lot different to the life of a football manager when you think about it, is it?"

Another character in the ongoing Channon horse opera who is in need of her daily adrenaline-kick is that other grand dame of his, Mrs Lesley White. She grins: "One of my very first memories of Mick still gets my adrenaline racing. In the old days he kept chickens on his farm and I was looking after his toddlers one day when the cockerel went for young Michael. Well, Mick panicked and gave that bird such an almighty kick that he sent it soaring up in the air and over the fence as if it were a football and he was taking a corner kick. But I'll say this for the cockerel – he came squawking back looking for more and Mick, being Mick, had calmed down by then and I'm sure he would have shaken hands with it if he could."

As unlikely as it may sound, Lesley's first job for Mick was as a babysitter. "I babysat for him and Jane the night Southampton won the FA Cup in 1976 and consequently I was at the stable to watch the birth of Royale Final with the rest of the family. My association with Mick began when he knocked on my father's front door one evening and asked him to look after a horse for him. My dad, Dick, and my mum, have a stud on the outskirts of Bishop's Waltham and Mick lived at nearby Waltham Chase at that time.

"Although Mick was already a young, local hero with the Saints, my dad had never met him before and he had no idea that Mick was into horses. So he got quite a shock to see this long-haired lad standing on his step saying: 'Hi, I'm Mick Channon' and then he came straight to the point by adding: 'I've got one yearling colt and a few yearling fillies. The time has come to wean them and I was wondering if my colt could run with yours.'

"Well, that little colt turned out to be Man On The Run, who was a multiple winner for Kevin [Keegan] and Mick. So right from the start it seemed that Mick was blessed with the golden touch when it came to horses. A good example was when his first horse gave birth to his winning colt, Jamesmead. Mick had thought she was barren but she ended up catching us all out by dropping Jamesmead in a field full of snow.

"Then, from minding Mick's babies, I went on to minding his horses. I used to break his yearlings for him, along with a couple of lads from his pal David Elsworth's stable. And when he finally decided to have a real crack at the training game, he took me down to Devon with him to work at the Bakers' yard. He just said: 'Come on gal, come with me, and we'll go right to the top together.' So it seems he knew how his fairy tale would pan out right from the beginning. As for my job description back then, well he just wanted someone to shout at, I think. But I had a wonderful time living with Rodney and Stephanie Baker.

"Mick's weekly party trick then was to race the stable lads for their wages every Friday evening. One of those lads is just down the road with Hughie Morrison now and he remembers it well. They were your usual crowd of mouthy teenagers and they used to be full enough of themselves to challenge the old footballer to this sprint every week. And although Mick was nearing 40 then, he used to beat them out of sight every time. He never, ever intended to keep their wages. So he had this ritual of buying their drinks afterwards and then giving me their money to pay them back next morning. But Mick being Mick, he still made them sweat every week by threatening that one day he was going to teach them a lesson by keeping the lot for himself, which he never did, of course.

"When Mick moved on to Ken Cunningham-Brown I moved there with him, too. And I've been with him ever since. He is not the easiest man to get along with but then I'm not the easiest woman, either. We have some right old swearing matches and I'll let you into this secret: the reason I go up north all the time is to keep out of his way.

"But seriously," adds Lesley, "if I didn't truly like and admire the man I would not have stayed with him all these years. For me, he is the best in the business. I think what he has achieved is second to none. From top footballer to top trainer has never been done before and never will be done again in my lifetime. Mick's special gift is that having been a top athlete himself, he understands the needs of his equine athletes. The most necessary quality a trainer requires is to understand horses and their special needs and Mick has that quality in spades. He can read their minds from the state of their bodies. He knows, from his own experience, what they can and cannot cope with, both physically and mentally. And he gives them tough love when that is necessary. I've never known a top trainer yet who wasn't hard on his or her horses occasionally."

CHAPTER THIRTY-ONE

JOKERS

There can be nothing more cold-blooded for one male – a trainer – to do to another – a horse – than to have him gelded. Well, there happens to be a joker in Mick's pack in the shape of middle-aged pedigree expert Tim Corby, who likes to relate amusing anecdotes to describe any situation – even a painful one such as this. As well as being a humorist, Corby is the jack of all trades in the Channon camp as he doubles up for Gill in the buying and selling department and for Lesley as the stable's travelling representative, a task that takes him on most of Mick's foreign raids. Not content with that, he also owns a couple of Mick's multiple winners from last season in Checkit and Tass Heel.

The gelding story that he so enjoys relating concerns a visit to the Doncaster sales seven years ago when he was buying a horse on Mick's behalf. He grins and says: "There's this little Scandinavian geezer in blinkers standing right next to me who keeps upping my bid in a broken English accent. This gives me the dead needle so I ring Mick on the mobile and ask him how high he's prepared to go for this particular animal and when he gives me my head I decide to take my foreign mate right to the wire.

"So the pair of us go at it bid for bid until, thank God, he eventually swallows it. But no sooner have I secured the horse than the Scandinavian - who turns out to be a Dane named Jurgen – offers me a profit on the deal and I tell him, appropriately enough: 'Bollocks!' As far as I'm concerned, that's it, job done. So I arrange for the horse to be boxed down to Mick's yard straight away and then I'm off home to Northamptonshire.

"Well, as soon as I'm up next morning, who's on my mobile phone but Jurgen. This time he's offering such silly money for the horse that I have to let Mick know about it again. But by now, Mick tells me, the vet has already arrived, first thing, and gelded the horse for jumping. I don't have the heart to tell Jurgen the colt is no longer an entire. But I promise to have a word with him anyway when I get to the sales again later that day.

"On the way back up to Donny I buy myself a bag of peanuts and put a couple of them in a jam jar in the car just to have a bit of fun with Jurgen about the horse being gelded and tell him that I hope he has no hard feelings about it. Well, we meet up in the bar there and he offers me what I consider to be crazy money for the horse. Then, never dreaming that I was going to get a result, I casually asked Jurgen where and when he would have run the horse had he beat me in the bidding and he only goes and says he would have had it gelded.

"'Oh, in that case,' I said, 'maybe we can still do business after all. He was absolutely delighted and said: 'I'll rush over to my bank right away.' And then he raises his glass to say: 'Cheers.' But I say: 'Don't say cheers; just say bollocks because you owe me an extra £150 in vet's fees 'cos we've already done the job for you.' And then I plonk the jam jar with the two peanuts in it down on the table in front of him and say: "There's the proof right under your nose." And with that I ring Mick and tell him to get the gelding boxed and straight back up to Donny before Jurgen changes his mind."

With a mischievous gleam in his eye, Corby then launches into another "iffy" story from his vast treasury of tales of the turf. This one concerns a horse of his called Shuffling and its Australian jockey Harry White who was nicknamed "Handbrake" Harry. In case you haven't already guessed the punchline, here it is:"The day Harry rode the horse, I didn't particularly want it to win off that handicap mark so he was lightly-trained. Shuffling went off at 50 to 1 and promptly pissed up, lightly-trained or not. What I didn't know, of course, was that Harry was going back to Australia the next day and had secretly decided to change the habits of a lifetime to acquire his fare back home from the bookies."

But Corby is not joking when he discusses the joint-ownership venture that he runs. "I choose partners who are in it purely for the sport and in brutal terms that means they have to be prepared to do their dough for the thrill of seeing their animals perform on the track. This type of ownership is for brave sportsmen and women who want to compete against the best occasionally because once in a while yours come up against animals who cost a fortune but couldn't beat me in wellies.

"I recently bought a decent animal for a crowd of lads who own dogs at Walthamstow. They want to have a pop at the gee-gees now and if they have a winner they can lord it a bit in their local pub can't they? I mean most blokes like to play Jack the Lad once in a while, don't they? And it can be done. For instance, I once gave 12,000 Irish punts for a little horse we called Innit after that catchphrase in the Ali G TV show. Well, she ran 15 times for us and won five of them. She won in Scotland, France and twice in Italy. As a two-year-old she won us prize money of £115,000 and we sold her to America for mega profits. And incidentally, she has already won a Grade Two race there for her new owners.

"Another little goldmine has been Checkit. I gave £24,000 for him at Doncaster as a yearling. In prize money alone, he won £147,000 as a two-year-old and £38,000 as a three-year-old. Then in January 2004 he was off to Dubai with eight others of Mick's top horses to race in the richest meeting in the world – the Dubai Racing Carnival, which carries total prize money of $21 million."

Another famous joker who pays fairly regular visits to West Ilsley is Frankie Dettori to ride work for the Sheikh Mohammed-owned horses stabled there.

One day in April 2003, as dawn was cracking its way through the frost on a morning that felt more like midwinter than spring, Frankie summed up what everyone else in racing feels at some time or another at that ungodly hour. He grumbled his way out on to the gallops after staying overnight at Mick's, saying: "The jokes we were sharing last night don't seem in the least bit funny now, do they?" Then he launched into the theme that is everyone's choice as far as Channon is concerned. "I've never had anyone swear at me as much as he does. But he forgets it a minute later." Smiling, Frankie then adds: "Some trainers are more reserved than Mick but none are more entertaining or better company. He has brought his language into racing straight from the football field, but there are one or two jockeys nowadays who can give him a run for his money when it comes to strong language, especially when they think you are trying to take their ground in a race."

Mick surprised Frankie on this occasion by asking him for his autograph. This turned out to be a request that was the prelude to one of Mick's saddest days last year. "The autograph," he says, "was for the grandchild of one of my owners, Neil Crook, who was a very close friend. Our wives and my kids and Neil's grandchildren were away together on holiday at that time.

"But he and I had a lunch date for an important race meeting at Newbury that day and Neil had rung me the previous evening with the request for Frankie. It was not until I arrived at the track with Frankie's autograph in my pocket that I received the news that Neil had died during the night of a heart attack.

"Neil was part owner of Imperial Dancer, of whom great things were expected that season. As it turned out Imperial did end up winning a Group One race but not until very nearly the end of the season. As I watched him win that race I was hoping that Neil had still got something to do with it wherever he was."

CHAPTER THIRTY-TWO

PARTNERS

Three of his stable's human-equine partnerships that Mick Channon will always remember with amusement and affection are those between Henry Ponsonby and Affair Of State, Doctor Michael Foy and Malapropism and Anthony Andrews and Knobbleeneeze. Upper-crust Ponsonby, who in the racing circles of the valley of horses is regarded as a Lambourn legend, was one of the first men to make a success of racehorse-owning syndicates.

As well as having some of his horses stabled at West Ilsley, he has them with Henry Cecil, Paul Cole and Fulke Johnson Houghton. Ponsonby has ancestors who were generals at the Battle of Waterloo and admirals at Trafalgar. But he admits to coming from the less well-heeled branch of the Ponsonby dynasty and having to begin his racing career as a humble stable lad. His main claim to fame in that pursuit is that, having joined Fulke Walwyn straight from school and then been sacked by that illustrious trainer, he returned 18 years later to ride a winner for the great man at Sandown. His claim to fame at West Ilsley is that his Affair Of State was the stable's first big winner. This filly won the Tattersalls Breeders Stakes in Ireland for the phenomenal prize money of 500,000 Irish punts 13 years ago and she still is Channon's biggest-ever prizewinner for a single race.

Henry says: "I bought the horse for a paltry £5,000 in Ireland at the time when this country was in recession and it was hard to sell shares in horses. A vet at the sales warned me off buying her because she had bad knees so I didn't bid. But the following day the vet returned to the sales to tell me that he had had a dream during the night that the horse would turn out to be something very special and this convinced me to go for her if she was cheap. Well, they don't come much cheaper than she did, so I took a chance.

"A mutual friend recommended that I put her with Mick and over a pint of Guinness I told him straight that he could have the horse not because he was a good trainer but because he was a famous footballer and it would be easier to sell the shares in her.

"At this, Mick exploded and said: 'What the fuck do you mean that I'm not a fucking good trainer? I'll soon show you how good I am.' And he swore even louder when he first clapped eyes on the horse. She was being broken in by Ben de Haan, who won the Grand National on Corbiere for Jenny Pitman and when we went to Ben's to see her, Mick was horrified. 'Look at those fucking knees on her,' he roared. 'They're worse than mine but the difference is I've got to train that fucker to run races with hers.' Then one day just after Christmas he astonished me by ringing up and saying: 'Get your arse down here quick. I've just put Richard Quinn up on the gallops and I can't believe my eyes. She's an absolute fucking cracker.'

"Early in the season we took her down the road to Salisbury for a little race for horses that cost £5,000 or less. I thought she was a certainty and had a big bet only to see her get beaten by a horse called Prince Ferdinand. I wasn't to know it then but

Prince Ferdinand was a splendid animal who went on to win at Royal Ascot.

"Two weeks later she pissed up in a maiden at Newbury and then we went to Royal Ascot with her for the Queen Mary and got Willie Carson to ride her. She finished stone last and Willie said she was a waste of time. But when the horse came back we discovered that she had a cough and was wrong. It was then that we decided to lay her out for the big one. Mick was courting Jill at the time and they came over to Ireland to watch her win. We had the mother of all craics and I went missing for four days. When I surfaced, Henry Cecil told me: 'Do you realise you've just won more prize money than the 1000 Guineas and 2000 put together?' And then I had to write cheques for £24,000 for Mick and £24,000 for Richard Quinn, who rode her despite Willie Carson's earlier assessment. One thing I'll always remember about that race is that Lester Piggott rode the second and I was shitting myself when he challenged us.

"Affair Of State is now a very successful broodmare; she's had eight winners, including a horse called Gun Salute who was bought by that ace winner, Sir Alex Ferguson."

Last season, Ponsonby was reported in some sections of the Press as being Sir Alex Ferguson's racing manager but he says that is not the case although he does confirm that Ferguson has a share in another of his syndicate horses, called Gatwick. Of his working relationship with Mick, Henry says: "There was a time when the likes of Mick used to doff their caps to the likes of me. Now, it is almost the opposite. I have ridden my horses work at his place and if he doesn't like what he sees the F-word comes thundering out and that cap of his goes straight down on the grass for a good kicking.

"I was riding out one of mine one day and when I'd finished I tapped gently on his office window. Mick looked up and said:

'What the fuck do you want?' I said I wanted somebody to take my horse off my hands. Mick went apeshit: 'Take your fucking horse? Take your fucking horse? You fucking get back out there and hose it down first and then give it a pick of grass.'"

Doctor Michael Foy is an orthopaedic surgeon who operates on the leading jump jockeys such as Tony McCoy, Mick Fitzgerald and Andrew Thornton, when they are injured in a fall. He first met Mick Channon as a patient when Mick went to see him about his bad legs. Michael says of their meeting: "I'd never had a patient like him before or since. My consulting room usually has a very quiet, almost cathedral-like atmosphere about it. But when Mick came in he was soon effing and blinding at the top of his voice. And when he gets excited or angry, which is often, he mixes up his words. So, for a bit of fun, I decided to call one of my horses after him by naming it Malapropism. That name, as I'm sure you know, is from a character in Sheridan's *The Rivals*, who was called Mrs Malaprop because she mangled her words.

"It so happens that one day at Bath last season I had a win double with this horse and another named Cauda Equina and this one got its name from a discussion I had with Mick one day about horses' tails and the human spinal surgery of that name. As far as Mick is concerned, though, the horse is called Cauda fucking Equina, of course. My wife, Denise, and I are very fond of the man – malapropisms and all. And professionally we've had great success with him, including a Group Two winner and the winner of a Listed race."

Actor Anthony Andrews and his wife Georgina are another couple who figure prominently in Mick's affections along with their delightful old character of a horse called Knobbleeneeze. Thirteen-year-old Knobbleeneeze is such a "Christian" that he was sent to the British Racing School to help teach young jockeys their chosen trade. Georgina tells the touching story of how she and Anthony came by this loveable character, who won 13 races for Channon and became one of his stable favourites. "Some years ago Anthony was working in Kentucky on an American film called, appropriately enough, *Bluegrass*," she says. "We had owned show horses but never a racehorse. But that all changed when we had this dream time visiting so many of the beautiful studs over there.

"Anthony bought a weanling who sadly came to nothing in racing terms, but whilst we were viewing this one I fell in love with an old mare who was 18 at the time and was only at the stud to pay off a bad debt, so the stud owner threw her into the deal for nothing. Her name was Proud Miss and she had been born in 1969. Back home with us she soon produced a foal called Transatlantic Dream. She looked so lovely that Ian Balding predicted a bright future for her but she turned out to be a transatlantic nightmare and finished up as a show hack.

"Miss's next foal for us was called Form Mistress. She also looked wonderful but unfortunately turned out to be useless. Her third foal for us was born when she was 21 and it was such an ugly duckling that the only thing for it was to call it Knobbleeneeze. Mick only had seven horses at that time and was renting a stable in Lambourn. And in Knobby's first race – at Goodwood – he looked destined to share the fate of his siblings when he veered across the course and was last by miles. But, amazingly, Mick had seen something there and said: 'I'll bet you a month's training fee this one will win before the end of the season. He lost his bet, but only by a few days because "Nobby" came out and won on the all-weather just after the season had finished. Incredibly, he went on to win more than £90,000 in prize money. And the strangest part of his fairy story is that he is the only winner we have ever owned, after more heartbreak horses than we care to remember."

Later that same year of 2003, in November, Mick also lost another great friend in Ted Bates, of whom he says. "As I've told you before, he was my mentor. He educated me at the university of life. I was virtually uneducated when I joined up with dear old Ted as a lad so anything I learned, I learned from him."

CHAPTER THIRTY-THREE

FAMILY

Michael Channon junior was in his mid-twenties when he stood in front of 150 people to give an oration at his paternal grandfather's funeral. Suddenly, he broke down in tears and could not continue. After a minute or two's pained silence, and with Michael still rooted to the spot in front of the congregation, his father, Mick, left his seat, went quietly up to his son's side and whispered in his ear: "OK son, kick on!"

Young Michael recalls that dramatic moment this way: "I adored my grandfather, Jack, so my emotions were all over the place. But dad's gesture got me out of trouble and I was able to continue my address." He tells this story to illuminate the macho way that his father expresses his love and concern. "We have never been a kissing, hugging kind of family and my old man has always been gruff when it comes to letting you know he cares. I suppose he got that way from spending a lifetime in football dressing rooms. But we can feel his sincerity. That's why we love him."

Another little classic anecdote in this vein is the one Michael tells about the time he broke his neck and was in intensive care, unconscious, for a long period of time. "It happened when I was a student at Bristol University. I had been sleepwalking – something I nearly always do when I've had too much to drink – and I managed to fall off a roof," says Michael with a grimace. "When I eventually came to I could gradually see the shape of dad hovering over my bed and, through the pain, I immediately thought: 'Oh no, he's going to give me the mother and father of a bollocking for being pissed.' But I couldn't have been more wrong. This was at the time of a long-running saga on *Coronation Street* when Ken Barlow was keeping an ongoing vigil on Deirdre in hospital. And the first words the old man said when I opened my eyes were: 'About time, too. I've been here so long that I feel like Ken fucking Barlow.'"

After making a complete recovery, Michael, who is 29, went on to obtain a degree in sports science and now works in television, where he recently produced a documentary on his father's life for Channel Four. He says of that experience: "It was weird because all I can see of my dad in my mind's eye is this balding, arthritic old heavyweight, but there he is on archive film quite skinny with long hair and waving his arm like a windmill every time he scores. But when I teased him about that windmill nonsense, he laughed and said: 'I should have patented that – I could have been a stone-rich lad by now, if I had done.'"

Of his present relationship with his father, Michael says; "Like a lot of fathers and sons, ours flourished when I grew up and we were able to have a pint together. And one of the first occasions this happened was when Dad married Jill and I was best man at the wedding. I remember it was the day John Major won the election in 1992. Dad had a few drinks at the reception and kept heckling the various speakers as if it was a political rally we were at."

Of his childhood, he says: "Dad was an absent father most of the time. To me, he always seemed to be away travelling round the world playing football. I was only about six when my parents split so I couldn't really take all that in. My sister, Nicky, and I stayed with our mum and she never ever says a bad word about dad. She even appeared with him on the *This Is Your life* TV programme when he was the subject of it a few years ago.

"I still live near my mum. She lives and works in Warrington and I live in Manchester, but we both travel quite a lot now. When I was a kid back down south, I played football and cricket for Hampshire schoolboys and I was keen to become a professional footballer at one time but having a famous footballer for a dad made me put too much pressure on myself. I'm still a keen Southampton fan, though, and travel to watch them whenever I can. I've never lost my love for Saints since dad took me to The Dell as a kid and introduced me to "uncle Alan" and "uncle Kevin" and the rest of those boyhood heroes. As for the horses, I haven't got around to them yet. They seem to take up too much time and study. Perhaps I'll switch to the gee-gees when I become an old geezer like the old man."

One Channon child who shapes up as if she might well take over the reins from her father one day, however, is his youngest – toddler daughter India, by his second wife, Jill. "She's a real livewire, that one," says her uncle Phil. "She's the one who makes sure Mick gets up at the crack of dawn every day to tend the horses by leaping on to his bed and insisting that he plays with her. She already loves the horses and she is a right tomboy who likes her own way. I can well see her taking over the stable from Mick one day. Her older brother Jack prefers football but he is studious and very intelligent, like his mother, and I can see him inheriting his father's business acumen."

But there is another Channon child who shows early signs of

rivalling India in the horse-loving stakes and that is Mick's grandson, Archie, who was at Goodwood when he was just a few months old to see Mick register his 100th winner of last season with a horse called Compton's Eleven. "Archie was gurgling away like a good 'un, watching his grandfather celebrate," says the baby's mother, Nicky, who, at 31, is Mick's eldest offspring.

Before giving birth to Archie, Nicky and her partner, Guy Morrall, had worked aboard multi-millionaire John Paul Getty II's luxury yacht, *Talitha G*, for the previous ten years. "When we started I was a stewardess and Guy was a deckhand, but now he is the captain and I am the purser," says Nicky proudly.

Nicky spent most of her working life entertaining Getty's celebrity friends who frequent the boat, but she says: "It makes me proud when they find out I am Mick Channon's daughter. Dad seems to be getting more and more famous every year."

When you've lunched with the Queen at Windsor, like Channon and his wife have, one assumes you can take celebrity in your stride – except that few people could resist name-dropping two of Mick's more recent lunch guests – Steven Spielberg and his actress wife, Kate Capshaw. "They came to visit us just after Archie was born and as Steven's company, DreamWorks, were the makers of the horse racing film *Seabiscuit* he and Kate were naturally keen to look around the stable," says Nicky. "Although what they made of it when dad's mum excused herself to go off and play bingo is anyone's guess."

Nicky takes typically Channon-like delight in telling the story of the one and only day her landlubber dad came aboard the boat – and promptly showed himself up. She recalls: "It was in Barbados where dad was on holiday with Jill and the children and we were tied up at Bridgetown. Our crew had clubbed together to buy a couple of modest horses called Wings Awarded and

Dashing Rocksville, which both won races, incidentally. Guy invited dad to come aboard, have a drink, and brief his new owners about their horses. We had only cruised three miles out of harbour when, in the middle of his pep talk, I could see my macho dad turning greener and greener and sweating up. It was a classic case of sea sickness and I had to rescue dad and get him back to shore before he died of embarrassment.

"Still, he is not in the least embarrassed when it comes to kissing and cuddling his grandson, though, except that he has trouble picking Archie up because that dreadful arthritis of his has spread to his wrists now. Mind you, he never complains. It's just not in dad's nature to whinge."

CHAPTER THIRTY-FOUR

STUD

Mick Channon stands gazing at the 120 acres of his very own Wiltshire greenery, oozing proprietary pride. He looks for all the world like a rancher in one of those *Big Country*-style Western films who is about to tell his heir: "All this will be yours one day." Such is his generous nature that it is certain that he will eventually want to gift this land to one of his nearest and dearest. It is situated just 20 miles from where he was born. The gentle rain is caressing horses who are scattered around in paddocks that look like the very essence of comfort zones for them. And he has an especially fond gleam in his eye as he watches a small herd of furry-coated foals frolicking to their hearts' content.

Then he says: "I can only hope that those young 'uns turn out to be as good as some of the excellent horses that have been bred here. The prestigious Meon Valley Stud kept mares here at one time and so did Phil Bull, the old-time form maestro." Channon bought this set-up last year when it was called Home Stud but it has since reverted to its original name of Norman Court. Add all this to the 400 acres he already occupies at his West Ilsley stable and you can understand it when he shudders just a little and muses:"I must admit that I do sometimes wonder if I've created a monster for myself."

This embryo "monster" is not necessarily of Mick's own making, though. For you can sense that subconsciously he feels that fate robbed him of a brother and that, consequently, it owes him all it is prepared to bestow upon him in return.

For instance, he says:"Just as I got that phone call to buy West Ilsley from out of the blue, a similar thing happened when I got my biggest break yet and out of nowhere I was sent a couple of Arab-owned horses. As it happened, they turned out to be almost useless so I thought I'd blown my chances of getting involved with the really big boys of this game.

"But then one dull, late-November afternoon that same year, when the rain was pissing down outside and I was in a mood to match the weather, I received a totally unexpected fax message informing me of my allocation of horses to be prepared for next season for Sheikh Ahmed.

"Well, as the racing world knows, they have been arriving every year ever since then and when you consider that they have included such stars as Bint Allayl, Josr Algarhoud, Tobougg, Queen's Logic and Zafeen I have been entrusted with the very best that money can buy or breed. Sometimes they get taken away at three and are sent to Godolphin which, after all, is Sheikh Mohammed's own baby, but that doesn't bother me. I am here to train horses; not to fall in love with them. I have to be as ruthless as a good soccer manager in that respect, although I must admit I did give my heart to Bint Allayl who was killed as the result of a training accident on the gallops and would have been an absolute monster had she lived.

"Last season was my best yet," says Mick of 2003, "but next

season could be even better now that I have this stud. This could turn out to be my greatest asset yet: it means that I will have control of my horses the whole year round. When they take a break here they are being fed the same as at the stable and they are in the same system, the same routine. When the Flat season is over we send our older horses here for a break or a holiday, if you like. And when any get injured they come here to convalesce. In some ways you could say that this is like a treatment room at a big football club.

"So, all things considered, I am more than hopeful of having another good season this time around. I am going to war again with some excellent horses. Majestic Desert is a very good filly indeed, Mahmoom and Seneschal have limitless potential too and Fun And Games could possibly stay well enough to win the Oaks and what a result that would be!

"I still think I can win a Classic one day. I am convinced of that. It might not be next year or the year after but it will come as long as I keep drawing breath, it will come. Meanwhile, I and my stable staff shall continue to get maximum enjoyment from all my winners and for as many of our owners as we can. We try to win for every one of them right across the board."

And when it comes to boards, you cannot get a much more power-packed list of racing names than some of those that appear on Channon's books, such as Sheikh Mohammed, Sheik Ahmed Al Maktoum, Salem Suhail, Jaber Abdullah, Robert Sangster and Peter Savill.

This must be what inspires him to declare: "I'm a rich lad now but that means nothing if you don't have a reason to get out of bed in the morning. Sometimes, I'm awake with excitement long before dawn at the prospect of what I'll be working with that day. Every punter likes to see a horse run fast and I'm no different because I'm still a punter at heart.

"But I can't stress strongly enough that it's not just the top-class horses that get my adrenaline flowing. Take Misternando, for starters. His progress has been nothing short of phenomenal. He was unraced as a two-year-old so he started off last season rated 46 and is now 101. He won most of his races by coming from behind and sometimes just scraping home. So that means we might still not have got to the bottom of him yet. Who's to say he can't improve another stone and turn up for the Ascot Gold Cup to challenge Elsie's great champion Persian Punch. Not many Flat horses can stay extreme distances like him so it may not be such an impossible dream as it looks on paper at the moment."

As for making his own impossible dream come true in such spectacular fashion, he says: "Well, I've had to check my stride, dive through a few gaps and change the whip hand a few times along the way but then that's what everyone has to do if they want to stay the course in life, don't they? I suppose the biggest change I've made, though, is in attitude. When the likes of Lawrie McMenemy first tried to discipline me, I was an argumentative arsehole. I used to tell him that I wasn't a brain surgeon or a rocket scientist – just a player.

"But as the years went by I learned that I had a duty to do the best by the talent I had been blessed with. And that if this meant learning to listen more then so be it. By that, I don't necessarily mean listening to opinions. Opinions just go in one ear of the person they are intended to impress and straight out the other, don't they? No, I mean by listening to other people's experiences and learning from my own. For me, experience is gold dust and the only way to gain a modicum of wisdom."

But then he laughs and snorts: "But you try stopping me from voicing mine, though. Seriously, I have to say that racing is the only sport in which you are penalised for winning and, even worse, for finishing second. But that's handicapping for you and we all know the rules.

"The trouble is you can't tell a poor old horse this when he is lumbered with an extra lump of lead in his saddle. Personally, I don't think there is such an animal as a racehorse that is not genuine. If they don't give their all you can bet your life there is something amiss with them and as the trainer it's your job to find out what it is. I mean, look at it from their point of view. We put bits of steel in their mouths, a little fella on their backs and expect them to do everything we want them to do. We breed them strictly for our pleasure, not theirs – although some stallions might argue that point. From my own experience as a professional athlete, I never over-train my animals. I say: 'Run them often, by all means, just like footballers who play twice a week, but don't grind them into the ground on the gallops.'

"I let them tell me how much work they need and, of course, it varies from individual to individual. Take one of my stable favourites, Muchea, he's what we used to call in the Southampton dressing room an old arse. He's been around for years, knows the routine and virtually trains himself. You know when his sort are coming good just by glancing at them. You can see it in their eyes and in their stride. But when they've woken up in a bad mood you can tell they are thinking: 'Fucking hell, I've got to go out on those gallops again when all I want to do is go back to kip.'

"On a going day, though, when old Muchea is standing up there next to a keen young colt, I can almost hear him giving the same advice that the old bull gave the young 'un when the young 'un said: 'See that herd of heifers up the hill – let's race up to them and shag one each.' And the old bull replied: 'No, let's stroll over there and shag 'em all!' Now, some people would call that tactics. But what are tactics other than a personal opinion."

Another way of describing tactics is to say that in reality they are no more than calculated guesses, which can quickly turn into unrealistic expectations, and can then become resentments under construction.

So, like the natural born winner that he is, Mick Channon will live the rest of his sporting life in hope rather than expectation. "That way you can dream as much as you want and you won't have to cry about any possible spilt milk later." For instance, in football, he would love to see Southampton win the Cup again during his lifetime or, even more surrealistically, finish top of the Premiership. But more pragmatically he will, just like any other true fan, always stay a believer no matter what.

He admits that he bowed, along with the rest of the Saints fans, in homage to that other, recently-retired, super Saint Matt Le Tissier. And he prays that the current, exciting, young Southampton striker, James Beattie, can clinch a place in the England squad for the Euro 2004 finals in Portugal this coming summer. "It would be sensational to see James score the winner for us that I could not manage to get against Poland all those years ago," he grins. Will he be betting on it? He says, circumspectly: "The only sporting certainty I know of is that if you don't buy a ticket you can't win the raffle – so what do you think?"

Well, by now I am so brainwashed by his omnipotence that I think I'll go out and have a long-range ante-post win-yankee on Southampton to do the double, England to win the World Cup, a Channon horse to land the Derby and his baby grandson, Archie, to be the first man on Mars. Oh, and on second thoughts, I'll probably make that a five-timer by backing myself to live long enough to collect.

For I happen to be privy to this Disney-like little anecdote that Mick's mother, Betty, told me. She maintains that the most excited state she has ever seen her middle son Michael Roger in was when, as a small boy, he came running home from a Saints match one day clutching a tuft of grass which he said he had jumped on to the pitch to grab after the final whistle. And then he solemnly asked his father to plant it in their garden, before predicting: "I'll be playing on a similar bit of grass to that down at The Dell one day…"

You'd have to be mad to bet against uncanny horse sense like that, wouldn't you?

MICK CHANNON'S FOOTBALL CAREER: 1965–1986

APPEARANCES

SOUTHAMPTON

SEASON	League	FACup	FLCup	Europe	Other	Total
1965–66 Div 2	3	0	0	0	0	3
1966–67 Div 1	1	0	0	0	0	1
1967–68 Div 1	27(1)	3(1)	1	0	0	31(2)
1968–69 Div 1	33	2(1)	4	0	0	39(1)
1969–70 Div 1	37(2)	3	2	5	0	47(2)
1970–71 Div 1	42	4	1	0	0	47
1971–72 Div 1	42	2	2	2	0	48
1972–73 Div 1	40	1	4	0	0	45
1973–74 Div 1	41	4	3	0	0	48
1974–75 Div 2	40	1	4	0	9	54
1975–76 Div 2	42	8	1	0	0	51
1976–77 Div 2	40	6	2	5	0	53
Totals	**388(3)**	**34(2)**	**24**	**12**	**9**	**467(5)**

GOALS

League	FACup	FLCup	Europe	Other	Total
1	0	0	0	0	1
0	0	0	0	0	0
7	1	0	0	0	8
8	1	3	0	0	12
15	2	1	3	0	21
18	1	1	0	0	20
14	2	0	1	0	17
16	0	2	0	0	18
21	1	1	0	0	23
20	1	3	0	5	29
20	5	0	0	0	25
17	3	1	4	0	25
157	**17**	**12**	**8**	**5**	**199**

MANCHESTER CITY

Season												
1977–78 Div 1	33(1)	0(1)	5(1)	1	0	39(3)	12	0	1	1	0	14
1978–79 Div 1	36	3	4	6	0	49	11	0	3	1	0	15
1979–80 Div 1	2	0	1	0	0	3	1	0	0	0	0	1
Totals	**71(1)**	**3(1)**	**10(1)**	**7**	**0**	**91(3)**	**24**	**0**	**4**	**2**	**0**	**30**

SOUTHAMPTON

Season												
1979–80 Div 1	37	1	0	0	0	38	10	1	0	0	0	11
1980–81 Div 1	42	4	2	0	0	48	10	0	0	0	0	10
1981–82 Div 1	40	1	2	4	0	47	8	0	0	1	0	9
Totals	**119**	**6**	**4**	**4**	**0**	**133**	**28**	**1**	**0**	**1**	**0**	**30**

CAROLINE HILLS (HONG KONG)

1982	Details not known

NEWCASTLE UNITED

Season												
1982–83 Div 2	4	0	0	0	0	4	1	0	0	0	0	1
Totals	**4**	**0**	**0**	**0**	**0**	**4**	**1**	**0**	**0**	**0**	**0**	**1**

BRISTOL ROVERS

1982–83 Div 3	4(5)	0	0	0	4(5)	0	0	0	0	0
Totals	**4(5)**	**0**	**0**	**0**	**4(5)**	**0**	**0**	**0**	**0**	**0**

NORWICH CITY

1982–83 Div 1	17(3)	0	0	0	17(3)	3	0	0	0	3
1983–84 Div 1	37	5	6	0	48	5	2	4	0	11
1984–85 Div 1	30(1)	5	8	0	43(1)	8	0	3	0	11
Totals	**84(4)**	**10**	**14**	**0**	**108(4)**	**16**	**2**	**7**	**0**	**25**

PORTSMOUTH

1985–86 Div 2	34	2	4	0	40	6	0	0	0	6
Totals	**34**	**2**	**4**	**0**	**40**	**6**	**0**	**0**	**0**	**6**

FINN HARPS

1986	Details not known

CAREER TOTALS

Southampton	507(3)	40(2)	28	16	9	600(5)	185	18	12	9	5	229
Manchester City	71(1)	3(1)	10(1)	7	0	91(3)	24	0	4	2	0	30
Newcastle United	4	0	0	0	0	4	1	0	0	0	0	1
Bristol Rovers	4(5)	0	0	0	0	4(5)	0	0	0	0	0	0
Norwich City	84(4)	10	14	0	0	108(4)	16	2	7	0	0	25
Portsmouth	34	2	4	0	0	40	6	0	0	0	0	6
Totals	**704(13)**	**55(3)**	**56(1)**	**23**	**9**	**847(17)**	**232**	**20**	**23**	**11**	**5**	**291**

ENGLAND & REPRESENTATIVE GAMES

	Apps	Goals
Southampton		
U–23	9	3
Full	43(2)	21
Football Lge	2	2
Totals	**54(2)**	**26**
Manchester City		
Full	1	0
Totals	**1**	**0**
GRAND TOTAL	**55(2)**	**26**

MICK CHANNON'S RACING CAREER: 1988–2003

1988

RACE DATE	HORSE NAME	COURSE NAME
16 February	Trout Angler	TOWCESTER

1989

26 September	You Know The Rules	NOTTINGHAM

1990

30 March	Wessex Warrior	WINCANTON
30 March	Golden Scissors	BEVERLEY
14 April	Cheveux Mitchell	KEMPTON
17 April	Slow Exposure	NEWMARKET
17 April	Pipers Hill	WARWICK
1 May	El Volador	BATH
21 May	Land Sun	WOLVERHAMPTON
5 June	Cheveux Mitchell	FOLKESTONE
7 July	Land Sun	BATH
20 July	Lustreman	AYR
8 August	You Know The Rules	KEMPTON
15 August	Cheveux Mitchell	SALISBURY
25 August	Golden Scissors	HEREFORD
29 August	Land Sun	REDCAR
31 August	You Know The Rules	SANDOWN
5 September	Dear Miff	FONTWELL
5 September	Golden Scissors	FONTWELL
11 September	Cheveux Mitchell	LINGFIELD
18 September	You Know The Rules	SANDOWN
2 October	Dear Miff	EXETER
11 October	Land Sun	HAYDOCK
12 October	Golden Scissors	MARKET RASEN
14 November	Wessex Warrior	KEMPTON

1991

8 March	Sleepline Fantasy	SOUTHWELL (A.W)
11 March	Beaujolais Nouveau	PLUMPTON
19 March	Beaujolais Nouveau	FONTWELL
23 March	Sunley Sparkle	LINGFIELD (A.W)
28 March	Sleepline Fantasy	BRIGHTON
1 April	Mighty-Q	WARWICK
8 May	You Know The Rules	SANDOWN
13 May	Coleridge	WOLVERHAMPTON
15 May	Cheveux Mitchell	KEMPTON
17 May	Affair Of State	NEWBURY
1 June	Cheveux Mitchell	LINGFIELD
8 June	Sunley Sparkle	EPSOM
15 June	Cheveux Mitchell	LINGFIELD
28 June	You Know The Rules	GOODWOOD
5 July	You Know The Rules	SANDOWN

RACE DATE	HORSE NAME	COURSE NAME
5 July	Misdemeanours Girl	SANDOWN
8 July	Miss Doody	LEICESTER
27 July	Sleepline Fantasy	ASCOT
13 August	Canadian Capers	BATH
24 August	Affair Of State	CURRAGH
24 August	Lustreman	HEREFORD
29 August	Miss Doody	LINGFIELD
14 September	You Know The Rules	DONCASTER
8 October	Standard Rose	NEWTON ABBOT
29 October	Silca-Cisa	REDCAR
19 November	Peatswood	NEWTON ABBOT
19 November	Trout Angler	NEWTON ABBOT
4 December	Grog	SOUTHWELL (A.W)

1992

8 February	Pleasure Ahead	LINGFIELD (A.W)
15 February	Pleasure Ahead	LINGFIELD (A.W)
10 March	Misdemeanours Girl	LINGFIELD (A.W)
23 March	George Roper	FOLKESTONE
27 March	Grog	BEVERLEY
28 March	Misdemeanours Girl	BEVERLEY
4 April	Grog	LINGFIELD (A.W)
1 May	Va Utu	NEWTON ABBOT
8 May	Va Utu	STRATFORD
30 May	Cheveux Mitchell	LINGFIELD
5 June	Marchwell Lad	GOODWOOD
10 June	Star Goddess	KEMPTON
12 June	Aradanza	SANDOWN
13 June	Canadian Capers	LINGFIELD
6 July	Miss Doody	RIPON
14 July	Misdemeanours Girl	BEVERLEY
20 July	Sunley Silks	BATH
23 July	Cheveux Mitchell	BRIGHTON
28 July	Felt Lucky	BEVERLEY
29 July	Silca-Cisa	GOODWOOD
30 July	Double Flutter	SALISBURY
12 August	Grog	SALISBURY
14 August	Mighty Miss Magpie	SOUTHWELL (A.W)
29 August	Lustreman	HEREFORD
31 August	Copy Lane	PLUMPTON
1 September	Clifton Charlie	RIPON
16 September	Latest Flame	BEVERLEY
21 September	Mr Butch	PONTEFRACT
24 September	Copy Lane	TAUNTON
5 October	Aradanza	PONTEFRACT
23 October	Copy Lane	EXETER
5 November	Knobbleeneeze	LINGFIELD (A.W)
12 November	Peatswood	TOWCESTER
16 December	Va Utu	LINGFIELD (A.W)

1993

RACE DATE	HORSE NAME	COURSE NAME
19 March	Va Utu	LINGFIELD
27 March	Mr Butch	DONCASTER
30 March	Va Utu	LEICESTER
8 April	Champagne Grandy	LEICESTER
19 April	Cyarna Quinn	MUSSELBURGH
20 April	Window Display	FOLKESTONE
23 April	Rohita	SANDOWN
17 May	Proud Brigadier	BATH
20 May	Rohita	GOODWOOD
20 May	Cheveux Mitchell	GOODWOOD
25 May	Waki Gold	FOLKESTONE
26 May	Domicksky	NEWBURY
7 June	Dodgy Dancer	NOTTINGHAM
8 June	Great Deeds	SALISBURY
12 June	Aradanza	YORK
12 June	Champagne Grandy	SANDOWN
18 June	Great Deeds	ASCOT
21 June	Kingswell Prince	PONTEFRACT
24 June	She Knew The Rules	SOUTHWELL
28 June	Princess Tateum	HAMILTON
13 July	Dodgy Dancer	FOLKESTONE
27 July	Dodgy Dancer	BEVERLEY
5 August	Cyarna Quinn	PONTEFRACT
6 August	Little Hooligan	SOUTHWELL
9 August	Knobbleeneeze	WINDSOR
14 August	Indefence	SOUTHWELL (A.W)
25 August	Henry's Luck	BRIGHTON
30 August	Indefence	NEWCASTLE
30 August	Henry's Luck	YARMOUTH
1 September	Va Utu	NEWTON ABBOT
10 September	Sixpees	GOODWOOD
11 September	Piccolo	DONCASTER
20 September	Domicksky	FOLKESTONE
23 September	Va Utu	TAUNTON
23 September	C D Shareplan	TAUNTON
25 September	Domicksky	HAYDOCK
4 October	Proud Brigadier	WARWICK
16 October	Champagne Grandy	CATTERICK
21 October	Strapped	PONTEFRACT
22 October	Glowing Jade	DONCASTER
26 October	Princess Tateum	REDCAR
30 October	Crazy For You	NEWMARKET
3 November	Champagne Grandy	BATH
10 November	Giggleswick Girl	LINGFIELD (A.W)
10 November	Rocality	LINGFIELD (A.W)
17 November	Peatswood	KEMPTON
27 December	Peatswood	KEMPTON

1994

RACE DATE	HORSE NAME	COURSE NAME
24 February	Princess Tateum	LINGFIELD (A.W)
26 February	Kelly Mac	LINGFIELD (A.W)
1 March	Kelly Mac	LINGFIELD (A.W)
15 March	Kelly Mac	SOUTHWELL (A.W)
22 March	Rowlandsons Gold	FONTWELL
25 March	Glowing Jade	DONCASTER
25 March	Poly Laureon	DONCASTER
26 March	Rigsby	DONCASTER
30 March	Champagne Grandy	CATTERICK
31 March	Gibaltarik	BRIGHTON
31 March	Knobbleeneeze	BRIGHTON
2 April	Springborne Lad	HAYDOCK
2 April	Great Deeds	HAYDOCK
2 April	Statom	KEMPTON
4 April	Poly Lane	NOTTINGHAM
14 April	Statom	NEWMARKET
14 April	Silca Blanka	NEWMARKET
22 April	Fantasy Racing	SANDOWN
26 April	Lady Davenport	BATH
2 May	Super Deeds	WARWICK
2 May	Double Flutter	WARWICK
6 May	Knobbleeneeze	LINGFIELD
7 May	Kelly Mac	BEVERLEY
7 May	Gone To Heaven	BEVERLEY
7 May	Al Corniche	BATH
9 May	Glowing Jade	REDCAR
14 May	Nordesta	LINGFIELD
25 May	Any One Line	BRIGHTON
30 May	Stato One	DONCASTER
1 June	Kelly Mac	BEVERLEY
1 June	Silca Blanka	EPSOM
3 June	Katya	CATTERICK
3 June	Domicksky	GOODWOOD
6 June	Oneineverycolour	NOTTINGHAM
10 June	Saint Express	YORK
10 June	Sweet Trentino	GOODWOOD
10 June	Fleet Hill	GOODWOOD
11 June	Statom	CAPANNELLE
13 June	Oneineverycolour	NOTTINGHAM
16 June	Princess Sadie	RIPON
17 June	Double Flutter	AYR
17 June	In Love Again	AYR
17 June	Sweet Trentino	NEWMARKET (JULY)
18 June	Dungeon Dancer	REDCAR
20 June	Double Flutter	MUSSELBURGH
25 June	Piccolo	NEWCASTLE
7 July	Fleet Hill	NEWMARKET (JULY)
9 July	Poly Amanshaa	LINGFIELD

RACE DATE	HORSE NAME	COURSE NAME
12 July	Giggleswick Gossip	FOLKESTONE
14 July	Pharsical	CATTERICK
15 July	Little Hooligan	WOLVERHAMPTON (A.W)
15 July	Kelly Mac	WOLVERHAMPTON (A.W)
19 July	In Love Again	FOLKESTONE
21 July	Mazeeka	HAMILTON
22 July	Mazeeka	CARLISLE
23 July	Scissor Ridge	WOLVERHAMPTON (A.W)
28 July	Welton Arsenal	SALISBURY
3 August	Mazeeka	BRIGHTON
4 August	Sumoquinn	BATH
9 August	Morocco	BATH
12 August	Sumoquinn	FOLKESTONE
17 August	Double Flutter	KEMPTON
18 August	Piccolo	YORK
19 August	In Love Again	SANDOWN
26 August	Pharsical	NEWMARKET (JULY)
29 August	Sumoquinn	CHEPSTOW
8 September	Sumoquinn	FOLKESTONE
13 September	White Lady	YARMOUTH
14 September	Musica	BEVERLEY
14 September	Princess Sadie	SANDOWN
16 September	Knobbleeneeze	NEWBURY
17 September	In Love Again	NEWBURY
1 October	Sumoquinn	NEWMARKET
1 October	Poly Laureon	WOLVERHAMPTON (A.W)
8 October	Sumoquinn	YORK
1 December	Home From The Hill	WINDSOR
15 December	Poly Road	SOUTHWELL (A.W)
27 December	Clifton Set	KEMPTON

1995

9 January	Poly Road	SOUTHWELL (A.W)
23 February	Home From The Hill	HUNTINGDON
2 March	Poly Road	LINGFIELD (A.W)
4 March	Poly Road	WOLVERHAMPTON (A.W)
27 March	Maggi For Marchgaret	FOLKESTONE
3 March	Cabcharge Striker	LEICESTER
1 April	Chastleton	WOLVERHAMPTON (A.W)
4 April	Dungeon Master	NOTTINGHAM
7 April	Jackatack	LINGFIELD (A.W)
8 April	Clifton Set	HEREFORD
15 April	Katya	KEMPTON
15 April	Rockforce	KEMPTON
17 April	Himalayan Blue	NOTTINGHAM
17 April	Poly Road	WARWICK
20 April	Dungeon Master	NEWMARKET
20 April	Danegold	RIPON
24 April	Satellite Star	BRIGHTON

RACE DATE	HORSE NAME	COURSE NAME
25 April	Arvzees	FOLKESTONE
28 April	Flying Squaw	SANDOWN
4 May	Yarn	SALISBURY
5 May	La Suquet	HAMILTON
9 May	Arvzees	DONCASTER
12 May	Indian Rhapsody	CARLISLE
12 May	Tadeo	CARLISLE
12 May	Giggleswick Girl	CARLISLE
18 May	Repertory	SALISBURY
25 May	Flying Squaw	GOODWOOD
25 May	Fantasy Racing	GOODWOOD
26 May	Arvzees	NOTTINGHAM
26 May	Musica	BRIGHTON
29 May	Whispering Dawn	CHEPSTOW
1 June	Giggleswick Girl	CARLISLE
2 June	Danegold	BATH
5 June	Satellite Star	HAMILTON
6 June	Pharsical	BRIGHTON
8 June	Champagne Grandy	CHESTER
8 June	Fantasy Racing	CHESTER
10 June	Silca Blanka	EPSOM
11 June	Cabcharge Striker	EPSOM
13 June	Champagne Grandy	SALISBURY
15 June	Indian Rhapsody	YARMOUTH
15 June	Halbert	HAMILTON
16 June	Danegold	GOODWOOD
16 June	Morocco	MUSSELBURGH
16 June	Giggleswick Girl	MUSSELBURGH
17 June	High Priority	BATH
23 June	Piccolo	ASCOT
29 June	Fantasy Racing	CARLISLE
1 July	Maggi For Margaret	DONCASTER
1 July	Pharsical	BATH
3 July	Halbert	MUSSELBURGH
4 July	Jambo	MUSSELBURGH
4 July	Sporting Fantasy	MUSSELBURGH
5 July	Solianna	CATTERICK
6 July	Rockforce	SALISBURY
8 July	Pharsical	CARLISLE
8 July	Fantasy Racing	CARLISLE
9 July	Cabcharge Striker	SAN SIRO
15 July	Marchtara	AYR
22 July	Maggi For Margaret	NEWMARKET (JULY)
31 July	Rockforce	RIPON
8 August	Fantasy Racing	BATH
16 August	Lady Caroline Lamb	CARLISLE
16 August	Morocco	CARLISLE
16 August	Maggi For Margaret	DEAUVILLE
21 August	Halbert	BRIGHTON

RACE DATE	HORSE NAME	COURSE NAME
21 August	Fantasy Racing	BRIGHTON
1 September	Flying Squaw	BADEN-BADEN
7 September	Knobbleeneeze	DONCASTER
9 September	Knobbleeneeze	GOODWOOD
13 September	Danegold	SANDOWN
15 September	Whispering Dawn	AYR
15 September	Champagne Grandy	NEWBURY
16 September	The Man	CATTERICK
26 September	Miletrian Refurb	BRIGHTON
2 October	Fantasy Racing	PONTEFRACT

1996

22 March	Hit Or Miss	DONCASTER
23 March	Kingsinger	DONCASTER
26 March	Miletrian Refurb	NEWCASTLE
27 March	Lady Caroline Lamb	CATTERICK
27 March	Muchea	CATTERICK
4 April	Champagne Grandy	LINGFIELD
8 April	Welton Arsenal	WARWICK
12 April	Sistar Act	NOTTINGHAM
16 April	Lady Caroline Lamb	FOLKESTONE
18 April	Statesman	RIPON
18 April	Muchea	NEWMARKET
2 May	Sunley Secure	HAMILTON
4 May	Braveheart	THIRSK
5 May	Kingsinger	SALISBURY
8 May	Vasari	CHESTER
9 May	Wait For Rosie	BRIGHTON
10 May	Recondite	CARLISLE
11 May	Poly My Son	BEVERLEY
16 May	Morocco	SALISBURY
20 May	Saunders Wren	WINDSOR
25 May	Statesman	KEMPTON
30 May	Corniche Quest	BRIGHTON
30 May	Dashing Rocksville	CARLISLE
31 May	Sistar Act	BATH
31 May	Cd Super Targeting	BATH
31 May	Ciserano	BATH
4 June	Stoney End	BRIGHTON
5 June	Lamorna	WARWICK
6 June	Knobbleeneeze	CHESTER
6 June	Russian Sable	GOODWOOD
12 June	Sistar Act	YARMOUTH
13 June	Irish Fiction	YARMOUTH
13 June	Bride's Reprisal	CARLISLE
14 June	Sunley Secure	GOODWOOD
17 June	Dungeon Princess	MUSSELBURGH
24 June	Maladerie	WINDSOR
3 July	Corniche Quest	YARMOUTH

RACE DATE	HORSE NAME	COURSE NAME
4 July	Victoria's Dream	HAYDOCK
7 July	Kingsinger	SAN SIRO
11 July	Recondite	NEWMARKET (JULY)
15 July	Sun O'Tirol	FOLKESTONE
22 July	Bride's Reprisal	MUSSELBURGH
22 July	Victoria's Secret	MUSSELBURGH
22 July	Saunders Wren	BEVERLEY
23 July	Silca's My Key	YARMOUTH
24 July	Poly Moon	CATTERICK
2 August	Dashing Rocksville	THIRSK
14 August	Hit Or Miss	HAMILTON
21 August	Lamorna	YORK
21 August	Silca Key Silca	AYR
22 August	Clifton Game	YARMOUTH
28 August	Levelled	CARLISLE
30 August	Muchea	BADEN-BADEN
17 September	Poseidon	SAN SIRO
19 September	Corniche Quest	YARMOUTH
19 September	Morocco	LINGFIELD
21 September	Blues Queen	AYR
25 September	Silca's My Key	GOODWOOD
21 October	Corniche Quest	FOLKESTONE
1 November	Whispering Dawn	NEWMARKET
5 December	Danegold	WINDSOR
20 December	Stonecutter	UTTOXETER

1997

11 January	Stonecutter	WOLVERHAMPTON (A.W)
31 March	Stately Princess	NEWCASTLE
31 March	Mile High	NOTTINGHAM
10 April	Levelled	FOLKESTONE
19 April	Rockforce	NEWBURY
26 April	Knobbleeneeze	RIPON
29 April	Cauda Equina	BATH
4 May	Golden Mirage	HAMILTON
9 May	Corniche Quest	CARLISLE
17 May	Fairy Domino	HAMILTON
19 May	Cauda Equina	BATH
23 May	Corniche Quest	NOTTINGHAM
24 May	Golden Mirage	CURRAGH
26 May	Henry's Mother	LEICESTER
6 June	Eponine	CATTERICK
7 June	Poseidon	DONCASTER
13 June	Flying Harold	CHEPSTOW
16 June	Levelled	BRIGHTON
24 June	Silca Key Silca	LINGFIELD
7 July	Cauda Equina	RIPON
22 July	The Honorable Lady	YARMOUTH
26 July	Sunley Seeker	SOUTHWELL (A.W)

RACE DATE	HORSE NAME	COURSE NAME
28 July	Jato Dancer	BRIGHTON
3 August	Gold Edge	CHEPSTOW
16 August	Rare Talent	RIPON
17 August	Corniche Quest	PONTEFRACT
17 August	Bay Prince	PONTEFRACT
20 August	Abajany	LEICESTER
20 August	Bay Prince	YORK
30 August	Take A Turn	CHESTER
8 September	Ajig Dancer	BATH
13 September	Danegold	BANGOR-ON-DEE
16 September	Abajany	SANDOWN
19 September	Knobbleeneeze	AYR
19 September	Sunley Seeker	NEWBURY
20 September	Lamorna	CATTERICK
22 September	Rare Talent	LEICESTER
24 September	Siena	GOODWOOD
27 September	Mrs Malaprop	CATTERICK
28 September	Levelled	BRIGHTON
4 October	Danegold	UTTOXETER
8 December	Cutting Anshake	SOUTHWELL (A.W)

1998

15 January	Classic Jenny	LINGFIELD (A.W)
16 February	Honey Storm	SOUTHWELL (A.W)
27 March	Inya Lake	DONCASTER
28 March	Poseidon	DONCASTER
4 April	Inya Lake	HAMILTON
4 April	Glen Ogil	HAMILTON
5 April	Muchea	CURRAGH
13 April	Queen Of Scotland	KEMPTON
13 April	Raffaello	KEMPTON
18 April	Golden Silca	NEWBURY
18 April	Silca Key Service	NEWBURY
21 April	Shanillo	FOLKESTONE
2 May	Chomper	HAYDOCK
4 May	Bride's Answer	KEMPTON
11 May	Palace Green	SOUTHWELL (A.W)
11 May	Wings Awarded	WINDSOR
14 May	Franco Mina	SALISBURY
15 May	Golden Silca	NEWBURY
16 May	Paula's Joy	THIRSK
18 May	Palace Green	SOUTHWELL (A.W)
19 May	Poco	BEVERLEY
26 May	Bint Allayl	SANDOWN
27 May	Knobbleeneeze	NEWBURY
5 June	Inya Lake	CATTERICK
12 June	Sunley Seeker	GOODWOOD
13 June	Captain Miller	LINGFIELD
16 June	Thank Heavens	THIRSK

17 June	Bint Allayl	ASCOT
27 June	Muchea	NEWMARKET (JULY)
1 July	Over The Counter	BRIGHTON
3 July	Silankka	HAMILTON
6 July	Diggit	BATH
8 July	Wings Awarded	FOLKESTONE
16 July	Morocco	LEICESTER
18 July	Golden Silca	NEWBURY
21 July	Abajany	BATH
21 July	Lokomotiv	YARMOUTH
25 July	Bundy	NEWCASTLE
25 July	Silankka	SOUTHWELL (A.W)
27 July	Danegold	YARMOUTH
31 July	Inya Lake	GOODWOOD
3 August	Maladerie	WINDSOR
4 August	Cauda Equina	BATH
5 August	Levelled	BRIGHTON
11 August	Abajany	AYR
19 August	Josr Algarhoud	YORK
20 August	Mrs Malaprop	SALISBURY
20 August	Bint Allayl	YORK
22 August	Levelled	LINGFIELD
29 August	Galapino	GOODWOOD
29 August	Danegold	CARTMEL
31 August	Over The Counter	NEWCASTLE
31 August	Danegold	FONTWELL
3 September	Cauda Equina	SALISBURY
4 September	Golden Silca	BADEN-BADEN
5 September	Maladerie	HAYDOCK
7 September	Cauda Equina	BATH
12 September	Danegold	BANGOR-ON-DEE
15 September	Sunley Sense	SANDOWN
15 September	Levelled	YARMOUTH
18 September	Thank Heavens	AYR
19 September	Sunley Sense	NEWBURY
19 September	Golden Silca	NEWBURY
21 September	Stately Princess	LEICESTER
23 September	Autocrat	CHESTER
24 September	Danegold	GOODWOOD
27 September	Autocrat	MUSSELBURGH
29 September	Maidaan	NEWMARKET
3 October	Danegold	CATTERICK
6 October	Galapino	FONTWELL
7 October	Maladerie	YORK
9 October	Danegold	ASCOT
12 October	Arcevia	AYR
4 November	Raneen Nashwan	MUSSELBURGH
17 November	Glastonbury	LINGFIELD (A.W)
21 November	Ranaan	WOLVERHAMPTON (A.W)
29 December	Questuary	LINGFIELD (A.W)

1999

RACE DATE	HORSE NAME	COURSE NAME
6 March	Cameo	WOLVERHAMPTON (A.W)
26 March	Danegold	DONCASTER
27 March	Ajig Dancer	WARWICK
29 March	Forty Forte	NOTTINGHAM
1 April	Captain Miller	LEICESTER
3 April	Inya Lake	HAYDOCK
3 April	Ma Yoram	KEMPTON
5 April	Master Fay	NEWCASTLE
5 April	Cote Soleil	NOTTINGHAM
5 April	Cotton House	WARWICK
7 April	Levelled	RIPON
10 April	Barringer	HAMILTON
10 April	Captain Miller	HAMILTON
10 April	Shakieyl	HAMILTON
15 April	Alfailak	NEWMARKET (JULY)
27 April	Barringer	NOTTINGHAM
28 April	Amsara	PONTEFRACT
29 April	Seazun	BRIGHTON
29 April	Mansa Musa	BRIGHTON
3 May	Master Fay	DONCASTER
4 May	Smart Ridge	BRIGHTON
6 May	Levelled	CHESTER
11 May	Areydha	YORK
14 May	Magic Grand	HAMILTON
15 May	Cd Flyer	THIRSK
17 May	Cauda Equina	BATH
17 May	Barringer	WINDSOR
26 May	Captain Miller	RIPON
27 May	Queen Of The May	BRIGHTON
1 June	Rowaasi	SANDOWN
7 June	Iyavaya	WARWICK
9 June	Magic Grand	HAMILTON
12 June	Term Of Endearment	BATH
15 June	Gin Oclock	THIRSK
18 June	Kalindi	ASCOT
19 June	Wadenhoe	AYR
25 June	Parkside Prospect	NEWCASTLE
30 June	Cauda Equina	BATH
5 July	Hunting Lion	BATH
9 July	Iyavaya	CHEPSTOW
14 July	Greyfield	FOLKESTONE
17 July	Wardat Allayl	NEWBURY
17 July	Master Fay	NEWBURY
19 July	Greyfield	BEVERLEY
20 July	Sioux Chef	BATH
23 July	Danegold	ASCOT
23 July	Joonayh	THIRSK
23 July	Sally Gardens	WOLVERHAMPTON (A.W)

RACE DATE	HORSE NAME	COURSE NAME
30 July	It's Allowed	THIRSK
31 July	Smart Ridge	HAMILTON
3 August	Otime	BATH
5 August	Smart Ridge	BRIGHTON
5 August	Ajig Dancer	BRIGHTON
6 August	It's Allowed	LINGFIELD
12 August	Natalie Jay	SALISBURY
14 August	Night Shifter	LINGFIELD
20 August	Greyfield	CHESTER
20 August	Cauda Equina	LINGFIELD
21 August	Inch Pincher	SANDOWN
23 August	Mehmaas	BRIGHTON
26 August	Shaman	FOLKESTONE
29-August	Ajig Dancer	YARMOUTH
4 September	Hunting Tiger	HAYDOCK
10 September	Doowaley	SAN SIRO
24 September	Miletrian	REDCAR
28 September	Seazun	NEWMARKET (JULY)
2 October	Cd Flyer	NEWMARKET (JULY)
16 October	Sheerness Essity	WOLVERHAMPTON (A.W)
3 November	Parkside Prospect	MUSSELBURGH
8 November	Queen Of The May	LINGFIELD (A.W)
11 November	Otime	LINGFIELD (A.W)
12 November	Tower Of Song	SOUTHWELL (A.W)
17 November	Makasseb	MAISONS-LAFFITTE
18 December	Parkside Prospect	LINGFIELD (A.W)

2000

26 February	Pedro Pete	LINGFIELD (A.W)
9 March	Greyfield	WINCANTON
6 April	Milly's Lass	LEICESTER
19 April	Ice Maiden	NEWMARKET
24 April	Roshani	NEWCASTLE
24 April	Dayglow Dancer	NOTTINGHAM
24 April	Imperial Dancer	WARWICK
2 May	Milly's Lass	NOTTINGHAM
2 May	Take Manhattan	NOTTINGHAM
2 May	Queen Of The May	WINDSOR
4 May	Blakeshall Boy	BRIGHTON
7 May	Innit	HAMILTON
8 May	Kachina Doll	WINDSOR
9 May	Soldier On	BRIGHTON
12 May	Take Manhattan	CARLISLE
18 May	Industrial Pride	SALISBURY
20 May	Budelli	LINGFIELD
22 May	Kachina Doll	BATH
24 May	Cd Europe	GOODWOOD
26 May	Joint Instruction	BRIGHTON
30 May	Cotton House	LEICESTER

RACE DATE	HORSE NAME	COURSE NAME
1 June	Piccled	GOODWOOD
3 June	Hunting Lion	NEWMARKET
4 June	King Silca	WARWICK
9 June	Golden Silca	EPSOM
9 June	Talaash	GOODWOOD
9 June	Follow Lammtarra	HAYDOCK
16 June	Lady Lahar	CHEPSTOW
16 June	Bint Habibi	CHEPSTOW
16 June	Shuwaib	GOODWOOD
16 June	Speedy Gee	SANDOWN
17 June	After The Blue	NOTTINGHAM
17 June	Cotton House	YORK
18 June	Aziz Presenting	SALISBURY
20 June	Cd Europe	ASCOT
22 June	Miletrian	ASCOT
22 June	Mazaarr	RIPON
23 June	Parkside Pursuit	REDCAR
1 July	Silca Legend	NEWCASTLE
7 July	Hotelgenie Dot Com	SANDOWN
7 July	Box Builder	SANDOWN
7 July	Shrivar	WARWICK
14 July	Your The Lady	CHEPSTOW
14 July	Pedro Pete	CHESTER
15 July	Karitsa	CHESTER
16 July	Industrial Pride	CURRAGH
20 July	Magical Flute	BATH
21 July	Roshani	NEWBURY
22 July	Ascension	NEWBURY
24 July	Your The Lady	BRIGHTON
25 July	Take Manhattan	BRIGHTON
26 July	Bint Habibi	LEICESTER
28 July	Pedro Pete	ASCOT
3 August	Soldier On	GOODWOOD
4 August	Fazzani	THIRSK
9 August	Blakeshall Boy	SANDOWN
11 August	After The Blue	SALISBURY
11 August	Fantasy Ridge	SALISBURY
11 August	Knobbleeneeze	SALISBURY
13 August	Carouse	LES LANDES
16 August	Shuwaib	DEAUVILLE
17 August	Ridgeway Dawn	SALISBURY
17 August	Natalie Jay	SALISBURY
20 August	Silca Legend	CHESTER
20 August	Golden Silca	CURRAGH
22 August	Imperial Dancer	YORK
25 August	Cauda Equina	BATH
26 August	Muchea	GOODWOOD
26 August	Lady Lahar	CURRAGH
26 August	Talaash	CLAIREFONTAINE

RACE DATE	HORSE NAME	COURSE NAME
27 August	There's Two	GOODWOOD
27 August	Cauda Equina	GOODWOOD
27 August	Ascension	DEAUVILLE
28 August	Joint Instruction	WARWICK
29 August	Makasseb	RIPON
30 August	Tobougg	YORK
2 September	Ridgeway Dawn	KEMPTON
2 September	Min Mirri	THIRSK
4 September	Joint Instruction	HAMILTON
6 September	Innit	DONCASTER
6 September	Miletrian	DONCASTER
7 September	Kalindi	DONCASTER
13 September	Nasmatt	YARMOUTH
13 September	Innit	MAISONS LAFFITTE
15 September	Soldier On	AYR
16 September	Tobougg	LONGCHAMP
18 September	Worthily	KEMPTON
21 September	Shrivar	PONTEFRACT
22 September	Piccolo Rose	LINGFIELD
23 September	Innit	SAN SIRO
29 September	Shrivar	NEWMARKET
6 October	Pedro Pete	YORK
8 October	Innit	SAN SIRO
9 October	Natalie Jay	LEICESTER
10 October	Samara Middle East	AYR
14 October	Tobougg	NEWMARKET
16 October	Worthily	PONTEFRACT
18 October	Digital	NOTTINGHAM
19 October	Greyfield	BATH
28 October	Worthily	NEWMARKET
3 November	Natalie Jay	DONCASTER
6 December	Knobbleeneeze	LINGFIELD (A.W)

2001

6 January	Makasseb	LINGFIELD (A.W)
27 January	Spartak	LINGFIELD (A.W)
24 March	Dayglow Dancer	DONCASTER
7 April	Lady Miletrian	MUSSELBURGH
3 May	Gold Guest	BRIGHTON
3 May	Fast Foil	BRIGHTON
6 May	Zinging	HAMILTON
7 May	Hakeyma	KEMPTON
18 May	Queen's Logic	NEWBURY
21 May	Blakeshall Boy	WINDSOR
22 May	Martha Daly	BEVERLEY
1 June	Addeyll	AYR
1 June	Tappit	BRIGHTON
6 June	Albania	CHESTER
8 June	Kulachi	GOODWOOD

271

RACE DATE	HORSE NAME	COURSE NAME
8 June	Parasol	HAYDOCK
9 June	Lupine	HAYDOCK
12 June	Royal Millennium	SALISBURY
16 June	Funfair Wane	YORK
16 June	Parkside Pursuit	BATH
20 June	Queen's Logic	ASCOT
25 June	Blakeshall	YARMOUTH
25 June	Anna Walhaan	NOTTINGHAM
27 June	Lady Lahar	HAMILTON
27 June	Parkside Pursuit	BATH
29 June	Blakeshall Boy	NEWMARKET (JULY)
30 June	King Carew	NEWCASTLE
1 July	Highdown	GOODWOOD
8 July	Arhaaff	NEWCASTLE
14 July	Aldafra	NOTTINGHAM
14 July	Kings Signal	NOTTINGHAM
14 July	Digital	YORK
14 July	Analyze	NOTTINGHAM
15 July	Dowhatjen	BATH
20 July	Kulachi	NEWBURY
26 July	Parkside Pursuit	BATH
26 July	Piccolo Party	BATH
27 July	Ya Hajar	ASCOT
10 August	Muffit	LINGFIELD
13 August	Sunley Scent	FOLKESTONE
15 August	Murrendi	YARMOUTH
17 August	Funfair Wane	NEWBURY
19 August	Sunley Sense	SANDOWN
23 August	Queen's Logic	YORK
24 August	Lipstick	BATH
25 August	Master Robbie	GOODWOOD
27 August	Aahgowangowan	RIPON
30 August	Natalie Jay	SALISBURY
3 September	Harnour	HAMILTON
7 September	Lipstick	KEMPTON
14 September	Fruit Of Glory	EPSOM
15 September	Dowhatjen	EPSOM
21 September	Harnour	AYR
22 September	Millennium Force	CATTERICK
2 October	Queen's Logic	NEWMARKET
3 October	Aahgowangowan	BRIGHTON
4 October	Aahgowangowan	NEWMARKET
6 October	Abajanuaryy	REDCAR
9 October	Simply The Guest	WOLVERHAMPTON (A.W)
11 October	Highdown	YORK
12 October	Pic Up Sticks	YORK
15 October	Imperial Dancer	AYR
22 October	Budelli	PONTEFRACT
30 October	Another Aspect	NOTTINGHAM

RACE DATE	HORSE NAME	COURSE NAME
7 November	Aahgowangowan	MUSSELBURGH
7 November	Harbour House	MUSSELBURGH
8 November	Another Aspect	WINDSOR

2002

19 January	Cotton House	LINGFIELD (A.W)
2 March	Double Fare	LINGFIELD (A.W)
9 March	El Pedro	WOLVERHAMPTON (A.W)
9 March	Dayglow Dancer	WOLVERHAMPTON (A.W)
22 March	Murray	DONCASTER
25 March	Double Fare	LINGFIELD (A.W)
30 March	Bravo Ragasso	KEMPTON
1 April	Imperial Dancer	KEMPTON
2 April	Khuzdar	SOUTHWELL
3 April	Machynleth	RIPON
5 April	Moon At Midnight	FOLKESTONE
11 April	Valiant Romeo	BRIGHTON
12 April	Basserello	CHANTILLY
19 April	Polar Force	NEWBURY
20 April	Queen's Logic	NEWBURY
20 April	Aramram	THIRSK
27 April	Analyze	LEICESTER
2 May	Dowhatjen	BRIGHTON
4 May	Aldafra	HAYDOCK
11 May	Washington Pink	BEVERLEY
11 May	Millennium Force	LINGFIELD
13 May	Sunley Scent	REDCAR
17 May	Albania	HAMILTON
17 May	Sticky Green	HAMILTON
18 May	Checkit	NOTTINGHAM
20 May	Scary Night	WOLVERHAMPTON (A.W)
23 May	Imperial Dancer	GOODWOOD
24 May	La Campanella	BRIGHTON
24 May	Checkit	PONTEFRACT
25 May	Silca Boo	HAYDOCK
25 May	Mail The Desert	WINDSOR
29 May	Digital	NEWBURY
30 May	Anna Walhaan	AYR
31 May	Ryme Intrinseca	BATH
31 May	Blakeshall Boy	BATH
1 June	Cd Flyer	KEMPTON
3 June	Sunley Scent	SANDOWN
9 June	Qazween	LINGFIELD (A.W)
10 June	Rileys Dream	NOTTINGHAM
11 June	Moujoudh	REDCAR
12 June	Kissing Time	BEVERLEY
18 June	Naahy	THIRSK
22 June	Moon At Midnight	AYR
24 June	Kissing Time	MUSSELBURGH

RACE DATE	HORSE NAME	COURSE NAME
26 June	Semigold	BATH
26 June	Diddymu	BATH
28 June	Vazon	FOLKESTONE
29 June	Bravo Ragasso	CHESTER
29 June	Peripheral	DONCASTER
29 June	Ashgar Sayyad	NEWCASTLE
30 June	Budelli	GOODWOOD
1 July	Fast Foil	WINDSOR
3 July	Just Say Yes	CATTERICK
3 July	Befriend	CATTERICK
3 July	Champion Lion	KEMPTON
6 July	Miss Ocean Monarch	BEVERLEY
7 July	Roskilde	REDCAR
7 July	Tusk	WARWICK
10 July	Londonnetdotcom	KEMPTON
11 July	Aries	FOLKESTONE
15 July	Imperial Dancer	AYR
18 July	New Wish	EPSOM
18 July	B A Highflyer	HAMILTON
19 July	Budelli	PONTEFRACT
19 July	Rileys Dream	PONTEFRACT
20 July	Miss Gigi	RIPON
22 July	Fruit Of Glory	WINDSOR
24 July	Kissing Time	LINGFIELD (A.W)
26 July	Budelli	ASCOT
26 July	Zafeen	SALISBURY
27 July	Millennium Force	NEWCASTLE
27 July	Fast Foil	REDCAR
27 July	Malapropism	REDCAR
27 July	Imperial Dancer	CURRAGH
3 August	Royal Millennium	GOODWOOD
4 August	Illustria	NEWBURY
4 August	Countess Miletrian	NEWBURY
5 August	Budelli	RIPON
15 August	Lady Zonda	SALISBURY
15 August	Sunley Sense	SALISBURY
18 August	Sunley Sense	KEMPTON
18 August	Cotton House	PONTEFRACT
18 August	Kissing Time	PONTEFRACT
21 August	Mardoof	CARLISLE
23 August	Queen's Victory	BATH
23 August	Sunley Sense	BATH
23 August	Sheriff Shift	THIRSK
23 August	Muchea	THIRSK
25 August	Naahy	GOODWOOD
30 August	Checkit	BADEN BADEN
31 August	Naahy	SANDOWN
1 September	Mail The Desert	CURRAGH
3 September	Ashgar Sayyad	YARMOUTH

RACE DATE	HORSE NAME	COURSE NAME
5 September	Roskilde	SALISBURY
6 September	B A Highflyer	EPSOM
6 September	Dayglow Dancer	HAYDOCK
6 September	Joint Statement	HAYDOCK
7 September	Jay Gee's Choice	HAYDOCK
11 September	Qazween	EPSOM
13 September	Joint Statement	GOODWOOD
14 September	Muchea	DONCASTER
14 September	Summerson	GOODWOOD
16 September	Joint Statement	BATH
17 September	Najeebon	YARMOUTH
20 September	Zafeen	NEWBURY
21 September	Dowhatjen	WARWICK
23 September	Valiant Romeo	CHEPSTOW
23 September	La Campanella	LEICESTER
23 September	Joint Statement	LEICESTER
25 September	Peripheral	CHESTER
28 September	Millennium Force	ASCOT
28 September	Lady Zonda	HAYDOCK
30 September	B A Highflyer	HAMILTON
3 October	Valiant Romeo	NEWMARKET
14 October	Fast Foil	WINDSOR
15 October	Craic Sa Ceili	AYR
15 October	Jay Gee's Choice	LEICESTER
17 October	Queen's Gift	SOUTHWELL (A.W)
19 October	Golden Silca	NEWMARKET
24 October	Joint Statement	BRIGHTON
26 October	Millennium Force	DONCASTER
26 October	Silca Boo	NEWBURY
7 November	Silver Buzzard	HAYDOCK
8 November	Fast Foil	DONCASTER
16 November	The Ring	WOLVERHAMPTON (A.W)
9 December	Senor Pedro	WOLVERHAMPTON (A.W)
14 December	Analyze	LINGFIELD (A.W)
31 December	Leonor De Soto	WOLVERHAMPTON (A.W)

2003

4 January	Tass Heel	SOUTHWELL (A.W)
4 January	Arry Dash	SOUTHWELL (A.W)
7 January	Senor Pedro	LINGFIELD (A.W)
24 March	Straw Poll	NEWCASTLE
4 April	Vigorous	FOLKESTONE
6 April	Millennium Force	CURRAGH
14 April	Najeebon	PONTEFRACT
14 April	Seneschal	WINDSOR
14 April	Arry Dash	WINDSOR
15 April	Naahy	NEWMARKET
16 April	Pic Up Sticks	BEVERLEY
19 April	Holborn	KEMPTON

RACE DATE	HORSE NAME	COURSE NAME
21 April	Mac Love	NOTTINGHAM
21 April	Majestic Desert	WARWICK
22 April	Pivotal Guest	NEWCASTLE
22 April	Black Falcon	NEWCASTLE
22 April	Analyze	NEWCASTLE
28 April	Vigorous	HAMILTON
29 April	Tusk	BATH
3 May	Almizan	THIRSK
8 May	Patandon Girl	FOLKESTONE
9 May	Fun And Games	CARLISLE
9 May	Digital	LINGFIELD
9 May	Aces Dancing	NOTTINGHAM
10 May	Tass Heel	BEVERLEY
14 May	Mokabra	NEWCASTLE
14 May	Kew The Music	NEWCASTLE
14 May	Night Wolf	NEWCASTLE
15 May	Master Robbie	SALISBURY
19 May	Silca's Gift	WINDSOR
21 May	Naahy	GOODWOOD
22 May	Cheverak Forest	NEWCASTLE
22 May	Fabulous Jet	NEWCASTLE
23 May	Rileys Dream	BRIGHTON
24 May	Catherine Howard	LINGFIELD
28 May	Master Robbie	NEWBURY
30 May	Malapropism	BATH
30 May	Nights Cross	BATH
12 June	Misternando	YARMOUTH
13 June	Dayglow Dancer	CHEPSTOW
14 June	Black Falcon	YORK
16 June	Master Robbie	WARWICK
17 June	Zafeen	ASCOT
20 June	Silca's Gift	ASCOT
21 June	Holborn	ASCOT
25 June	Black Oval	SALISBURY
26 June	Ryme Intrinseca	HAMILTON
26 June	Fast Foil	SALISBURY
27 June	Pennyghael	FOLKESTONE
28 June	Bravo Dancer	NEWCASTLE
1 July	Breezit	BRIGHTON
1 July	Leonor De Soto	BRIGHTON
2 July	Misternando	YARMOUTH
3 July	Cd Flyer	HAYDOCK
4 July	Beauty Of Dreams	BEVERLEY
4 July	Nights Cross	BEVERLEY
4 July	Scotch N' Dry	SALISBURY
5 July	Naaddey	BEVERLEY
5 July	Cedarberg	CHEPSTOW
5 July	Zap Attack	CHEPSTOW
6 July	Sahnour	REDCAR
10 July	Jimmy Byrne	NEWMARKET (JULY)
10 July	Leonor De Soto	WARWICK

RACE DATE	HORSE NAME	COURSE NAME
11 July	Master Robbie	ASCOT
11 July	Misternando	CHEPSTOW
14 July	El Pedro	WINDSOR
17 July	Waaedah	EPSOM
19 July	Happy Holiday	HAYDOCK
19 July	Futoo	RIPON
21 July	Arfinnit	AYR
21 July	Top Seed	BEVERLEY
24 July	Tusk	DONCASTER
24 July	Truly Wonderful	SANDOWN
26 July	Fabulous Jet	NEWCASTLE
26 July	Tolzey	NOTTINGHAM
28 July	Hoxne Star	YARMOUTH
29 July	Imperial Dancer	GOODWOOD
1 August	Dontstopthemusic	NOTTINGHAM
1 August	Misternando	NOTTINGHAM
2 August	Joint Statement	THIRSK
4 August	Budelli	RIPON
5 August	Saida Lenasera	CATTERICK
8 August	Mac Love	HAYDOCK
11 August	Kristiansand	FOLKESTONE
13 August	Misternando	SANDOWN
16 August	Tusk	NEWMARKET (JULY)
16 August	Mokabra	RIPON
17 August	Londonnetdotcom	BATH
17 August	Mac Love	KEMPTON
21 August	Misternando	FOLKESTONE
23 August	Cd Flyer	GOODWOOD
23 August	Malapropism	GOODWOOD
23 August	Majestic Desert	CURRAGH
25 August	Cheverak Forest	RIPON
26 August	Misternando	RIPON
26 August	Compton's Eleven	YARMOUTH
29 August	Analyze	AYR
29 August	Master Robbie	AYR
4 September	Irma La Douce	CARLISLE
5 September	Millbag	HAYDOCK
5 September	Mokabra	BADEN BADEN
6 September	Fabulous Jet	HAYDOCK
12 September	Jazz Scene	DONCASTER
12 September	Checkit	DONCASTER
12 September	Compton's Eleven	GOODWOOD
13 September	Muchea	DONCASTER
13 September	Digital	GOODWOOD
13 September	Najeebon	GOODWOOD
13 September	Misternando	GOODWOOD
15 September	Tass Heel	MUSSELBURGH
16 September	Cairns	SALISBURY
16 September	Le Tiss	SALISBURY
18 September	Almizan	AYR
20 September	Imperial Dancer	AYR

RACE DATE	HORSE NAME	COURSE NAME
23 September	Mahmoom	NEWMARKET
25 September	Muchea	GOODWOOD
26 September	Fabulous Jet	HAYDOCK
27 September	Master Robbie	ASCOT
28 September	Le Tiss	MUSSELBURGH
28 September	Flotta	MUSSELBURGH
1 October	Millbag	SALISBURY
4 October	Tusk	NEWMARKET
5 October	Nights Cross	TIPPERARY
6 October	Princess Anabaa	PONTEFRACT
7 October	Tass Heel	CATTERICK
9 October	Master Robbie	YORK
11 October	Najeebon	YORK
11 October	Naahy	YORK
12 October	Khuzdar	BATH
12 October	Cheverak Forest	NEWCASTLE
13 October	Makfool	AYR
17 October	Mahmoom	NEWMARKET
18 October	Tass Heel	CATTERICK
18 October	Cairns	NEWMARKET
21 October	In The Pink	YARMOUTH
24 October	Bravo Dancer	DONCASTER
24 October	Flotta	DONCASTER
24 October	Misternando	NEWBURY
24 October	Royal Millennium	NEWBURY
25 October	Imperial Dancer	NEWBURY
31 October	B A Highflyer	BRIGHTON
1 November	Fun And Games	NEWMARKET
5 November	Malapropism	MUSSELBURGH
5 November	Misternando	MUSSELBURGH
13 November	Fools Entire	LINGFIELD (A.W)
16 November	Imperial Dancer	CAPANNELLE
8 December	Lyrical Girl	SOUTHWELL (A.W)
29 December	Wood Fern	LINGFIELD (A.W)

INDEX

The index is arranged alphabetically except for subheadings, which appear in approximate chronological order.